WHAT PEOPLE ARE
SAYING ABOUT
ANNEMARIE SHROUDER

"Annemarie Shrouder is truly a thought-leader in conversations of diversity and inclusion. The paradigm shifts and empowerment I've gotten from working with her have brought our organization to a whole new level. Understanding and embodying best-practices in this critical field is a fast route to greater influence and profitability."
— *Teresa de Grosbois, International #1 Best Selling Author, Founder: Evolutionary Business Council*

"The quality of Annemarie's facilitation is outstanding. She was able to guide and lead the conversations to bring everyone into the discussion. The group itself was extremely diverse, and at times, it could have broken down into problematic conflict. Annemarie was able to lead discussions away from problems without preventing people from participating and without cutting off discussion. A good facilitator improves a meeting or session. A great facilitator draws so much value from everyone in the room that you end up getting far more, in far less time, than you ever thought possible. Annemarie is a great facilitator."
— *Robert A Hubbs, MarTech Expert, Coaches Coach*

"I had the opportunity to see Annemarie present a several-hour presentation on race and ethnicity and how racism has permeated our society in ways we aren't even aware. The subject was a difficult one but was handled expertly and with lots of insight by Annemarie and her co-presenter. Her even-handed ideas and thoughts in an area that could easily have been explosive was exquisite."
– *Sharon McGrill International #1 Bestselling Author*

"A lot of conversation [happened] after the work-shop, which raised the awareness with our partners that we have to do more work in this area. They didn't realize how big of an impact it would have… Annemarie talks the talk and walks the walk. People believe what she is saying. She is genuine and compassionate. She comes to this work from a very natural and respectful way."
– *Margaret Seko*

"Annemarie is able to create a space where all of us with varying levels of knowledge and understanding of these issues can learn and share our knowledge without feeling judged."
– *Ikem Opara*

"We felt that Annemarie was someone who could hold us accountable in a good way, not in a way that was going to make us walk away feeling blame and shame, like this is work we all need to do. And it's ok to be uncomfortable. Annemarie has been blessed with the ability to do this work and to speak and write the experiences and the emotions that can be sometimes too overwhelming for us to express.

– *Dionne Martin*

BEING BROWN IN A BLACK AND WHITE WORLD

Conversations for Leaders on Race, Racism, and Belonging.

ANNEMARIE SHROUDER

Hardcover: 978-0-9958292-7-5
Ebook: 978-0-9958292-6-8
Paperback: 978-0-9958292-8-2

A NOTE FROM ANNEMARIE

Hi!

Thanks for picking up this book, for being curious or excited or intrigued.

Thank you for recognizing your part in creating a world where people of *all* skin colours feel a sense of belonging.

Whatever the reason, thank you for being here!

More than Diversity & Inclusion

Diversity and Inclusion (D&I) are popular these days. Everyone seems to be talking about it; there are chief diversity officers, chief inclusion officers, D&I managers. Company commitments to diversity and inclusion are on their websites; organizations are more conscious of the images they use.

And yet, we don't seem to be much further ahead "on the ground" where it matters: people's *experiences*.

Part of the reason is that I don't believe we *really* know what we are talking about. Diversity simply means difference, all kinds. Inclusion is a feeling. It's about our experience.

Verna Myers said, *"Diversity is like being invited to the party. Inclusion is like being asked to dance."* It's a beautiful analogy because if you've ever been to a party and stood there awkwardly, well, it doesn't feel good. Being there doesn't really matter if you're not part of the action.

This started as a book to support D&I.

And, it still is.

But in order to do D&I well, we have to change our conversation about "race."[1]

"Race" is not real.

It's a social construct, which means that someone made it up.

And that fact means that we are more similar than we think and have been taught.

If we *really* want things to change, if we want to create spaces where people belong, feel included, feel welcomed, are more engaged, and are really contributing, and if you as a leader are *really* committed to diversity and inclusion, to really connecting with people from all walks of life, we have to be able to hold space for *both/and* rather than *either/or* which polarizes us especially around the issue of "race."

As leaders, we need to be willing to step into that space, open up to the truth about "race" that keeps us separate, and make ways to see more in order to create a new way of being together: one where people are truly seen, heard, and valued. Now, that's a *real* party!

Sharing this book with you is a bit scary, to be honest.

---

[1]   Race isn't a real thing. It's a social construct invented by people some hundreds of years ago. So, when I used the word, it will be in quotation marks.

Because the only way I could share this message in a meaningful way (rather than as an intellectual exercise) was to make it personal, which means I had to be willing to be vulnerable and "show up." And showing up can be scary.

I'm excited to take you on this journey, to share with you what I have learned, and am learning, and to introduce you to the bridge I am committed to creating around issues of "race."

Capitalization

In equity, anti-oppression and anti-racism circles, the words black and people of colour are often capitalized. I believe it's about making a point regarding our humanity which is often discounted, overlooked and unacknowledged. I have been capitalizing these words for years and I recently read that a major US news outlet changed their practice and started capitalizing black.

I also have noted that in two of my most recent reads (Michelle Obama's book *Becoming* and Isabel Wilkerson's book *Caste* - both incredible and important) the words black and people of colour are not capitalized.

Then my editor asked me about it, and I had to pause.

The spirit of this book is both/and. And in that spirit, capitalization of skin colour (some but not all) feels off. Therefore, I have made a conscious decision to make black and people of colour (as well as white) lowercase. So that we can have a conversation without the capital lording it over us. To give us a chance to see each other better, really, finally as all human beings with different amounts of melanin. Lack of melanin has been used by people who are white to feel and act superior (consciously and unconsciously). The results have been nothing short of devastating and horrific for black people - particularly in the United States of America, but also in Canada and around the world. If the capital in any way suggests that those with more melanin should have a go at feeling superior (rather than acknowledged, as I believe it was intended) then it will derail the both/and conversation.

This isn't about flipping power; it's about *sharing* space and power. Finally.

People First Language

Another thing you may notice in these pages is people-first language: people who are black rather than black people. This is not my creation, but it's an important change that I believe helps us to remember that we are people first, and that skin colour is one way that our diversity is visible.

Get Ready for Something Different!

This book is probably a little different than any other D&I book you've picked up. Well, *I'm* a little different, so this is a unique approach. Writing it this way was the only way I could share this work with you that feels authentic, present, and meaningful.

This work is so important, and I wanted to show up on the page.

So as a leader, you may be shocked, confused, maybe awed (hopefully not dismayed) to learn that this book has poems.

I'll give you a moment.

I know; why poems in a leadership book about "race," inclusion, and belonging?

Don't be scared. They aren't "airy-fairy" or wildly academic, and they do not require intellectual gymnastics or a dictionary to comprehend. They are simply the way my heart speaks and the clearest way I know to share these messages with you.

The poems you will read are the insights along my journey. They have helped me see more, grapple with pain, helped me understand, and helped me to heal.

It is my hope that these poems take you to your emotions, and by doing so, create a bridge to a new way of seeing and a new way of being—as a leader and with your people. And I hope this is a way that inspires awareness, belonging, connection, and the creation of a culture where "race" is understood for what it is, so everyone is seen, heard, and valued.

Why Leaders?

I'm passionate about working with leaders because when *leaders* "get it", cultures shift and people thrive.

I'm inspired by the willingness, the vulnerability, and the openness with which I have seen great leaders lead. When we add an inclusion lens and the courage to talk about "race," we have gold.

I invite you to check out my Inclusive Leadership Program at:

http://annemarieshrouder.com/inclusive-leadership-program

Wherever you are at – if this is your first foray into D&I and your first conversation about "race" or if you're already wading through these and live them every day—welcome.

Here we go!

Annemarie

FOREWORD

By Rodney Patterson

Shrouder's provocative reveal in *Being Brown in a Black and White World*, reminds me of a quote one of my mentors used frequently. It was from his daughter Freda, who was known to say, "Dad, sometimes I feel like a loose strand of hair in a wig shop." Shrouder reminded me of how many of us who identify as black, come to accept how we are viewed in the world, often relegated to the bottom of the social strata. Still, we take comfort in being able to claim a group and to some degree, a culture. We identify with a specific group of people who overcome and persevere, black people. Those who identify as white, share a similar experience, albeit at the other end of the social strata. *Being Brown in a Black and White World* opens our eyes to those individuals who identify as biracial and multiracial. These are the individuals who often feel like Freda, a loose strand of hair in a wig shop.

For many years, I have been intrigued by the experiences of people who identify as biracial and multiracial. In the late 1980s, I served as Director of Multicultural Affairs at the University of Vermont. Many students viewed the Multicultural Center as a safe haven. Some ventured in reluctantly because of their personal struggles with their racial identity. I conducted several interviews with these students. In *Being Brown in a Black and White World*, Annemarie Shrouder has afforded me a peek into the minds and hearts of that in-between community, that has been often overlooked or altogether, forgotten. Comparatively, this work taught me so much more than I learned 30 years ago.

Shrouder has written a gem. In *Being Brown in a Black and White World*, she does more than join the chorus of voices affirming that race is not real; she dares to posit that race is a fabrication designed to appease those who profited from the Trans-Atlantic slave trade. You will appreciate the transparency with which she shares her most personal struggles and passionate insights. As invited voyeurs, she escorts us along a tumultuous journey, balancing her narration between story-telling and poetic interludes.

While *Being Brown in a Black and White World* is not intended solely for corporate audiences, she masterfully makes the content relevant. Shrouder invites the reader to consider critical questions after each chapter, challenging us to move from an exclusionary either/or mindset to an inclusive both/and reality.

Being Brown in a Black and White World is a personal invitation to experience liberation through the lens of one who has been liberated. I believe you will be as moved and honored as I to have shared this experience with her. Enjoy the journey.

Rodney S. Patterson,
CEO, The Learner's Group; Pastor, Shiloh MBC Chicago; Author, "Trumping the Race Card: A National Agenda, Moving Beyond Race and Racism"

FOREWORD

. . . .

By Candy Barone

I still remember the moment when Annemarie Shrouder, who at the time was attending a workshop of mine, uttered three words that forever changed my life.

We were in the middle of a deep conversation within the group, where the topic of racism was brought to light, and I said, "I don't see colour."

Annemarie then responded, "That's the problem."

I found myself triggered. *What!?* I thought to myself. *What was that supposed to mean?*

It was only after I spent some time with what Annemarie shared with me, stepped into that trigger, and asked her to explain more that I began to realize what she meant.

I. Don't. See. Colour.

You see, I grew up as an Air Force brat, and I was surrounded by diversity. I used to say that my group of friends was like the United Colors of Benneton, so how could I possibly be someone who disregarded the disparity, the truth, all around me?

How could I be part of racism and the culture it created?

I thought I couldn't possibly be one of *those* people. I did work with inner-city kids; I engaged in diversity projects. I even created a violence prevention program within the Milwaukee Public School District. I didn't see colour because I felt we were all the same; *all lives matter.*

Sound familiar?

I took great pride in my blinders. I thought in seeing us all as the same that I had risen above the impact and effects of racism.

However, those three words cut like a knife that day. I. Don't. See. Colour.

I started to do deep inner work to ask myself why I was so triggered by Annemarie's statement. It wasn't like she attacked me with those words or judged me. There was no anger in her words. In fact, there was a neutrality and calmness to what she spoke. A simple yet profound truth that woke me up at the core of my being. I. Don't. See. Colour.

She spoke those three words to me more than three years ago. Since then, I've spent a lot of time reflecting, leaning in, and doing the hard work.

Why didn't I see colour? What was I missing in not seeing colour?

The answers were profound. Once I began to *see* colour, I couldn't unsee it. I saw how different life was for those who were white like me, with privilege, versus those who were black or brown.

I began to see the systemic nature of how colour is used as a measure, as a mechanism, to further separate, discriminate, and marginalize those who have darker skin and melanin than I do.

Then May 25, 2020 happened. The incident that shook the entire world. The moment we all witnessed a black man die at the knee of a white police officer that shot across social media and the news. In eight minutes and 46 seconds, we saw the breath of George Floyd be taken from his body.

I knew that I would never be the same. It was like a spark. I wanted to be educated, had to be educated, on the full impact of systemic racism, and how our colour-blindness was exactly, as Annemarie shared with me years ago, the very problem. I wanted to be a voice and amplify the voices of those who had not been heard for so long.

I leaned in even more and realized that we all have a tremendous amount of unpacking to do. We carry stories, conditioning, and trauma in our bodies and unconscious. We have biases that we have never questioned or explored at deeper levels. We have been blind to the ways systemic racism has been embedded into everything (e.g., our schools, our churches, our communities, and our organizations).

Now is the time to come face-to-face with those biases and to dismantle the very systems that oppress, discriminate, and marginalize. It's time to take responsibility and unpack it.

One of the things that I love most about Annemarie's work is that she brings a different approach to begin the unpacking process (or continue, depending upon where you are in your own journey).

Through her use of poetry, she is able to speak a deeper, more intimate, and vulnerable truth. She shines such a beautiful and powerful light on the questions, the beliefs, the difficulties in not belonging, in not fully being seen.

Through her journey of both/and, we, as readers, can feel her truth, imagine the possibilities, strip down our own blocks, biases, and barriers, and begin to engage in a different type of discussion. The both/and mentality changes the conversation to one of compassion, empathy, and love, one where we choose to *see* colour and embrace it, one where we celebrate the differences and create cultures and environments of equity and inclusion, and one where we lean in and lead differently, with purpose, with grace.

I was so honored when Annemarie asked me to write the foreword for this book. This exquisite masterpiece in which she shares the rawness and realness of her journey, of her heart.

As I worked in the corporate sector for 20 years in my career, and now still facilitate leadership trainings and workshops across many different organizations, I believe that the power of being able to see colour and to embrace the both/and conversation is one that will change the landscape and soul of business forever.

And, it is work we need to embrace and engage in now.

Racism is a leadership conversation. Leadership is a choice. It is a responsibility we all share. It's time to do the hard, uncomfortable work to break down systemic racism in our communities and, most definitely, within our organizations.

This book is a great place to begin.

For we have, right now, the opportunity to create real cultures of diversity, equity, inclusion, and equality in the workplace. And, it starts with each one of us.

Thank you, Annemarie, for shining a light, for speaking your truth and for sharing your heart. And, thank you for loving me enough to help me truly see colour.

Candy Barone, leadership development trainer, coach and speaker
CEO & Founder, You Empowered Strong

CONTENTS

. . . .

WHY THIS BOOK IS RIGHT ON TIME

This book has had many iterations. And it is right on time because I have landed in the place where I can write it outside of the pain, in a place of healing.

Plus, the world changed as I wrote this second draft in the summer of 2020. The killing of George Floyd by police in Minneapolis, Minnesota, USA, on May 25, sparked protests, and an awakening among people who are white. The conversations I have been having since with leaders feel different. And I have hope that we can make a significant impact, realizing that likely this leaning in won't last.

I have done diversity and inclusion, and anti-oppression work for over 16 years with over 40 organizations.

I have seen and experienced what happens when I approach this work from a place of anger or frustration, and I have seen and experienced what happens when I approach this work with love and compassion.

I intentionally choose the latter. It's a hard bridge to create sometimes, but I believe it is necessary if we want things to be different.

Inclusion ROI

What difference can it make when we really see people for who they are and what they have to offer, *as well as the context we live in?*

Some of the key outcomes associated with greater inclusion and belonging are:

Increased:

- Engagement
- Satisfaction
- Productivity
- Innovation

Leadership is the key to inclusion because people show up more—literally and figuratively—when leaders create cultures where people:

- Feel safe, connected, and seen
- Can learn together
- Can have tough (and real) conversations about the things that really matter to them and impact them
- Feel a sense of belonging

It is in that showing up that the magic happens—for you, your people, and for your bottom line.

Talking about "Race"

This book is right on time because we have started to crack open around issues of "race" and racism in North America in these last few years. "Race" isn't real by the way, it's a concept created by someone centuries ago to categorize and ascribe value based on skin colour. It then made it easier for people who are white to accept the transatlantic slave trade that dehumanized African people. And, as Isabel Wilkerson clearly outlines in her book *Caste*, it was then used to create a caste system on which the United States of America has been built.[2] Because "race" is a social construct, I have chosen to put it in italics throughout this book, as a reminder.

Racism—the systemic manifestation of the belief that people who are black and people of colour are inferior to people who are white - on the other hand, is very real.

As I wrote the second draft of this book in the summer of 2020, we were experiencing a heightened level of awareness about systemic anti-black racism and systemic anti-racism. People who are white were wanting to learn about "race" and racism in a way I have not seen in my lifetime but in a way that gives me hope.

This new consciousness makes it more possible to *really talk* about "race" and racism and to imagine a new way—a way that acknowledges where we have been, and what is (and points to) what *could* be if we do this work well.

---

[2]   Canada can be included in this caste system, although I have yet to find as powerful a book about it.

One of Einstein's quotes is: "No problem can be solved from the same level of consciousness that created it."

Although much of the consciousness that continues to perpetuate inequities around "race" is unconscious, **the time for a new consciousness around "race" and racism is now.**

Look around. It's already happening. We need to keep going.

As a "biracial" person, the struggle I see in the world and in organizations around issues of "race" (consciously and unconsciously) has been playing itself out in my body and my life:

- The push and pull
- Having to choose—or being told it's necessary
- A win/lose mentality
- Never allowing/creating space for **both**

There are fewer and fewer spaces where we can come together (even physically now, in the era of COVID-19). Although we tell ourselves we are doing better in the areas of diversity and inclusion, we are not.

We are becoming more and more polarized.

The gap is getting wider.

Because the work I do with organizations and in the world is what I have experienced in my body, I know that the gap will break us if we don't make a change.

(Cue Michael Jackson's "Man in the Mirror" here *"…if you want to make the world a better place, take a look at yourself and make a change…"*)

This is why I'm so passionate about connection: connecting people, building community, creating spaces where people have a sense of *belonging*. And why I'm passionate about helping people "see more"—more of themselves, each other, and situations. I believe it's how we will heal the racial divide.

These are my stories and accompanying insights into the workplace and the impact of "race" and racism.

I offer them to you in order to shed some light, crack you open to the myth of "race," and support a new way of seeing and looking at each other.

And in order to support my hope for something new.

Welcome.

I'm glad you're here.

WHY THIS BOOK? (THE SH*T JUST GOT REAL)

This is not the book I wanted to write.

And this is not how I wanted to write it.

It was supposed to be a "business book."

What you are holding is my personal story with "race" that I share with you in order to help heal our racial divide, so workplaces can become safer places where people of all skin colours can show up, be all of who they are, and are seen and acknowledged for what they have to offer.

This book is a book for leaders.

Because conversations about "race" require leadership and leaning in by leaders *like you*, whether you are a CEO, an ED, a VP, a director, a manager, or someone who leads without an official title.

This book is also about my life. I use my stories to illustrate the racial divide and its impact not only on me personally but also as an illustration of the larger impact.

If you're uncomfortable as you read parts of this book, *that's okay*.

"Race" and racism are painful for *all* of humanity. "Race" is something someone made up, and the uptake of that idea has been wreaking havoc for centuries on people who are black and brown physically, and on all of us spiritually.

In my work with clients, "race" is a place few have wanted to go, at least until June 2020. We need to see, acknowledge, and understand what "race" and racism are and what they mean for each of us and for *all* of us. Regardless of the colour of our skin, where we live, or where we work, this separation we have created has an impact.

I hope that my words will be a bridge that allows you to connect with people, to *remember* that we are all connected, and to move forward together in meaningful ways—representing the myriad of colours in the human palette.

Sharing My Story

This book has been in me for a long time. The title has been with me for a long time.

I have tried to write other books, but this one kept nudging its way in.

So, here it is.

I'm terrified. Being vulnerable is scary. But the time for hiding is over. No more.

I feel there will be people who are black who may read this and say, "Who is she to be writing about "race"? She doesn't know what it's like to be black."

You are right.

This is *my* story.

I am not black *or* white. And as a "biracial" individual, I have some insights into both sides.

So *that's* who I am to be writing about "race" and moving forward.

I am a bridge.

Poems are the way I write with my heart, and that was important to me, so that's why they are included throughout this book. I didn't want this to be a solely intellectual exercise; inclusion requires the heart *and* the head. I wanted to *show up* on the pages. I wanted you to see me, feel the pain, the joy, the confusion, the heartbreak, the healing, and the hope. My hope is for you to begin to understand that what we have been doing around, with, and within the concept of "race" is not working, and join me in creating something new.

I've written about my life and my experiences—both personally and professionally. I hope they provide some insight into why it's important to lean into these conversations as a leader.

Real issues. Real talk. Real change.

WHAT THIS BOOK IS...AND ISN'T. AND WHO IT'S FOR.

. . . .

This is not a how-to book.

It's not a book that will tell you how to do diversity and inclusion work (or even anti-racism work since it seems to have hit the mainstream now) in your organization or company.

It won't teach you how to talk about "race."

But it will *help* you to do these things, and do them *better*.

It also doesn't present you with steps. And it's not a workbook.

This book is meant to show you a new way of being with and seeing "race."

We must learn to talk about "race" in a way that shows understanding, compassion, and healing.

We must learn to do diversity and inclusion and anti-racism well, *meaningfully*.

We must learn to deeply connect with people and build a culture of belonging.

When *we see more, we can do better*.

How engaged are your employees?

How do they feel when they walk into work?

What *else* do they have to offer that your organizational culture may be blocking?

How well do your employees know each other?

How aware are employees who are white about the impact of "race" and racism on their colleagues who are black and brown?

Catalyst released a report in 2016 that highlighted the emotional tax black employees face in the workplace and the impact on their health, and their contributions.[3]

How aware are employees who are white about the impact of "race" and racism on their lives?

A new and different awareness and understanding around "race" and racism is how we will create something new, something better, together.

This is a book for leaders who are courageous, who are daring, and who "get it."

Leaders who *truly* want to create better representation at all levels, more diversity, greater inclusion, healthier cultures, and happier people.

It's for leaders who want to make a *real* difference in not only *who* is in their organization but also what *positions* those people hold and how their people *feel*.

We spend a lot of time at work. And I work to create change within companies and organizations. But leadership extends beyond workplace titles, and beyond the workplace.

This book is for leaders who understand that organizations mirror society, and that we have work to do.

So, let's get started!

---

[3]   https://www.catalyst.org/wp-content/uploads/2019/01/emotional_tax_how_black_women_and_men_pay_more.pdf

CHAPTER 1

Either/Or (When You're not One or the Other, What are You?)

This book started many years ago as a title and an idea, or rather a feeling of not having a place to belong.

I was born in Montréal, Québec, Canada, in 1970 to immigrant parents.

My mother is from Austria. My father is Jamaican. Both had found their way to Montreal in their early 20s, for different reasons, to "start a new life."

As someone who is "biracial," I was never black enough for the black kids, and I wasn't white. What that has meant for me is an energy of either/or—an energy that to me, for most of my life, felt like nothingness.

Nothing

As a kid
I think I'm nothing
not black enough for the black kids

Not white

Too brown for Austria
Too light for Jamaica

I race back and forth
trying to find a place
that is mine
that will claim me

"Come and rest,"
it will say
"Here
with us.
We want you…"

It's a place I never find

Tired
weary
feeling empty
and never enough

Unless I am nothing

And then I can manage
to float
unseen

But that hurts too

In my family, "race" dynamics played themselves out between my Oma[4] and my dad. I could feel the divide as a very young child and took it upon myself to fix it in the only way I knew how.

---

[4]   Oma is one of the German words for Grandmother. My Oma was my maternal grandmother.

Do You Like...?

One of my
childhood pastimes
is running
between two sides

Checking to see
if the animosity I feel
is real
or imagined

If it's safe

If there will be peace

"Dad, do you like Oma...?"

But the bookends
of my life
(one black,
one white,
both forces
to be reckoned with)
are not in accord

"Oma, do you like Dad...?"

BEING BROWN IN A BLACK AND WHITE WORLD

Each time
the answer is yes
or sure
or a laugh
meant to dismiss

I know it isn't real

If they like each other
I won't have to pick
a side

What I am coming to understand, through the work of Isabel Wilkerson[5], is that the *structure* of the racial divide is about caste. Reading about history with this lens has shed a deeper and clearer light and insight into human behavior and interactions around "race". It is also helping me to further my understanding of that knot in my stomach as a child, and that almost imperceptible (and not articulated) contempt I could sometimes feel in my Oma.

Picking Sides

Ultimately, my life experience has been about feeling like I have to pick. The result has been a life-long ping-pong game trying to align myself with each side, in turn, and depending on the context.

Culturally, this has been easier than visually. My mom was a stay-at-home parent for most of my life. This meant that I learned German (Austrian dialect, actually), and we spent whole summers in Austria every five years or so when I was a child—long enough to cultivate relationships with my cousins and become pen pals in a pre-internet world.

We always lived in neighbourhoods with predominantly white demographics. I went to schools with mostly white student populations. In fact, I distinctly remember wanting to go to the local public high school when we moved to Mississauga when I was 12. It felt like it would be more *exciting*, which for me was all

---

[5]   Isabel Wilkerson's book: *Caste – The Origins of our Discontents.*

about the fact that the building looked like the high schools I saw on TV and that there were more black kids. My dad told me in no uncertain terms that I would not be going there. Instead, he registered me in a separate school with a uniform because he felt there would be more discipline. He was probably right, but what that meant was that I was one of a handful of kids of colour. I'll write more about that later.

While this is my story, my father was also finding his way in the corporate world as a black man. This meant experiencing subtle and overt racism in the workplace in the form of lower expectations, enduring racist comments, and having his knowledge questioned and his capabilities challenged. He also faced several barriers in finding work when we moved to Ontario in 1982. A few years after that move dad eventually ended up in the C-Suite. Based on the numbers today, I believe he could even have been one of the first black people to be C-Suite in Canada.

But it didn't come without challenges.

"Among Fortune 500 companies, <u>less than 1% of CEOs are black</u>. Today there are only 4, down from a high of 6 in 2012, according to Fortune. And over the past two decades, there have only been 17 black CEOs in total. Of those, only one has been a woman -- Ursula Burns, who ran Xerox from 2009 to 2016.

But among Fortune 100 companies this year, black professionals account for just 3% of CEOs, 1% of CFOs and

3% of profit leaders like division presidents, according to the <u>Stanford Corporate Governance Research Initiative</u>.[6]

Living in a White World

White is a world I was and am comfortable in; I get how it works. That may sound strange to you if your skin is white, but if you are a person of colour or black, I know you'll understand what I mean.

The world people of colour live in, especially people who are black (North American or Caribbean, given my context and experience), has always felt foreign to me. And it has been a source of private pain and even shame.

[6]   https://www.cnn.com/2020/06/02/success/diversity-and-black-leadership-in-corporate-america/index.html viewed: September 13. 2020

The Bus Stop (Things You "Should" Know, if You're Black)

Grade 3

My best friend
is Nicole

She is black

She introduces me
to the Jackson 5
and
The Little River Band
which we sing
at the back of the class
when the teacher isn't watching

"Friday night, it was late, I was walking you home…"

Her parents are from Trinidad
her home is an oasis

New smells
hair products in the bathroom
a joy I can't place
an energy I drink in
music is always playing
I learn about Motown

Nicole teaches me
the Bus Stop
possible access

to a part of myself
I have yet to discover

I feel a momentary hope

But it's fleeting

If I was black enough
I wouldn't need the Bus Stop

I would be able to dance

My father has been very present in my life, and I know and love things like ackee and saltfish, codfish fritters, breadfruit, and bami. Christmas isn't Christmas without Sorrell[7]. I know who Miss Lou[8] is and listened to her poetry on an LP. But I have always felt there was a gap between my paternal cousins and me, between my Jamaican family and me. One week of vacation every five years or so doesn't allow for relationship building, and shared love for Milo and D&G pineapple soda isn't a strong enough foundation for pen pals.

To me, black culture, the black world (in all its diversity), has always felt like something I watch with my nose pressed against the glass; it's close enough to see up close but not to touch and experience. I keep wishing that I could break through, that my skin was darker to allow entry and my knowledge deeper to allow me to sink in.

This is a pain I have carried my whole life. Despite my new focus and "place" of both/and, I still feel it. Although less, it still creates a lump in my throat and the pinprick of tears behind my eyes. What have I missed? I will never know.

It's not just my colour that has kept me apart. It's experience and immersion; my life. It's the invisible barrier created by either/or. But that gap has always felt like a

---

[7] All of these are Jamaican foods, and Sorrell is a drink.

[8] Miss Lou is a Jamaican cultural icon; poet, actress, social commentator, comedienne, folklorist and singer. For more information: https://www.nlj.gov.jm/archives/Miss_Lou/index.html (viewed Dec. 30/20)

shortcoming, like I was not enough. I always wished I was darker skinned, that I was "more black."

In the world we now live in, since George Floyd was killed by a police officer in Minneapolis and the ensuing protests (and subsequent shootings)[9] and spotlight/ leaning in to understand anti-black racism, my story feels different. The pain I have felt feels like it mirrors the pain I see in the world: either/or, us/them. That's not new[10], but the leaning in by people who are white is new. The curiosity is new, the willingness to listen and learn is new. And people searching for knowledge are watching US documentaries like *13th* or Canadian documentaries like *The Skin We're In* by Desmond Cole.

This willingness and curiosity will help to heal the racial divide if these are accompanied by action for real change that will dismantle systemic anti-black racism. Either/or is where we have been living for centuries, since "race" was created as a social construct, the US caste system was created, and racism was born. Both/ and is the energy I am stepping into, and inviting others to consider, so we can listen, share, learn, and move forward together.

The Polarizing Impact of "Race"

The challenge with either/or, black or white, is that it leaves no room for the middle.

---

[9]   https://www.cbsnews.com/pictures/black-people-killed-by-police-in-the-us-in-2020-part-2/

[10]   https://www.cbsnews.com/pictures/black-people-killed-by-police-in-the-u-s-in-2020/84/

"Race" is extremely polarizing. In my experience, people feel that they have to take sides. An examination of US laws over time will show that who was considered white and who was considered black changed, to suit those in power (people who were white). I include myself in this feeling of having to take sides because I felt that way for most of my life. What happens then is that each side creates a circle (figuratively) and turns in towards each other, excluding the other side. There is history, of course, that suggests this is prudent (for protection) for people who are black: 400+ years of individual and systemic racism and a caste system that helped to build the United States of America and Canada, for example. That same history taught people who are white to insulate themselves and consider themselves superior by dehumanizing people who are black.

That turning in and away from results in "us and them" thinking, which leaves little to no room for building connection, creating opportunities for dialogue, to hear and be heard or to really see the other and be seen. What we have then is what we are experiencing now particularly in North America, and even more obviously in the USA, where people who are black and people who are white have generations of division, and the chasm continues to get wider. Because we focus on either/or. And in an either/or world, someone has to win, and someone has to lose.

That happened in my family. It happened in my body.

In organizations, I see either/or thinking manifesting in the following ways:

1. Leadership that is white-skinned, and front line that is brown and black-skinned

   When looking at statistics from the USA, where black people make up 12% of the population, the numbers are dismal; African Americans make up 3.2% of senior leadership roles and 0.8% of Fortune 500 CEO positions[11]. If you add gender and look for statistics on black women, the number will be lower. It's no better in Canada; we just don't collect data as well.

2. Differential treatment—interviews, employment reviews, how people are managed, and access to promotion (to name a few)

   In my own work with organizations, focus groups consistently result in data that shows that employees who are black or of colour have negative experiences with interviews, are offered lower positions despite experience or education, are micromanaged, deal with microaggressions at work, and are less likely to be promoted, despite experience or education. It's no wonder that the Centre for Talent Innovation's report *Being Black in Corporate America* suggests that doubts about diversity and inclusion efforts have black Americans opting out of the corporate hustle.[12]

---

[11] https://www.cbsnews.com/news/black-professionals-hold-only-3-percent-of-executive-jobs-1-percent-of-ceo-jobs-at-fortune-500-firms-new-report-says/ read April 29, 2020

[12] https://www.nytimes.com/2019/12/09/us/black-in-corporate-america-report.html Read April 29, 2020

3. Differential experiences in terms of support, safety, and trust

Again, it has been my experience that employees who are black or of colour are more likely to experience the workplace as lacking in support, safety, and trust than their white colleagues.

Skin colour is a major contributing factor in someone's experience globally. Because of systemic racism, these experiences tend to be negative for people of colour (particularly for those who have skin that is black) and positive for people who are white-skinned.

To be clear, many of these differential experiences are not necessarily because of behavior that is conscious. In fact, either/or thinking is so deep and so old that I would suggest much differential treatment due to skin colour is now unconscious and part of a broken system (a caste system) where we assume these faulty beliefs to be true and "the way it is," which further impacts our ability to examine and question them. The belief that "race" as a real thing is a perfect example of this.

The unconscious perpetuation of racism is not an excuse, and it doesn't hurt any less, but it's a reality that we live in societies where either/or thinking is rampant in the media, curriculum, and in our day-to-day conversations. And so, we pick it up whether we intend to or not. We will continue this discussion in the next chapter. For now, I leave you with a few questions.

Questions to Ponder

1. Consider your workplace representation. How does the representation look for people of colour and people who are black in entry-level positions? How about in management? Senior management? Executive level? What do you notice as the trend in your organization?

2. If you do employee engagement surveys, how are people *feeling* about the work climate based on their skin colour? (If you don't ask or don't ask for demographics so you can disaggregate the data, consider starting. You are missing an opportunity to see people and the impact of their identities and to create change.)

3. If you don't do employee engagement surveys, why not?

Either/or is painful for everyone. Both sides suffer as a consequence.

Either/or keeps us away from holding both/and as a possibility and as a reality. And that is where the magic is, as you will see.

CHAPTER 2

Microaggressions and Systemic Racism: Messages that Tell You what "Side" of Either/Or You are On

Microaggression is a term coined by Professor Chester M. Pierce in 1970; although in my experience in the field of Diversity & Inclusion (D&I), it's only been taken up in the last decade or so, and more so now. Dr. Pierce created this word to describe the daily verbal insults and dismissals that African Americans were subject to by white Americans.

Since then, we have expanded the definition to include the recognition that all Historically Disadvantaged Groups[13] experience these verbal insults and dismissals by those in dominant groups (groups with social power).

---

[13]   *Historical disadvantage: disadvantage resulting from historic patterns of institutionalized and other forms of systemic discrimination, sometimes legalized social, political, cultural, ethnic, religious and economic discrimination, as well as discrimination in employment. This also includes under-representation experienced by disadvantaged groups such as women, Aboriginal peoples, persons with disabilities, LGBT*

In my work, microaggressions are important for people to understand, be able to catch, and then speak up against in the creation of inclusive workplaces. However, microaggressions can and do happen everywhere and anywhere. Regardless of the location, their message is clear—you are different, and you don't belong. Like racism (and any ism), they travel along the lines of power, from those who have social power to those who do not/have less. And they teach us our "place"—who belongs, and who does not.

Examples of Microaggressions

"You're so articulate!"
"Where are you from?"
"Can I touch your hair?"

Microaggressions chip away at one's sense of belonging and remind everyone of the gap between either/or, us and them, that keeps us from connecting in our shared humanity. Isabel Wilkerson shares 8 pillars of caste in her book, all of which are designed to make and keep the hierarchy intact and remind people of where in the hierarchy they belong. The fact that microaggressions come wrapped in a seemingly complimentary package highlights the systemic nature of racism and the ways

---

persons and racialized people. Source: http://www.ohrc.on.ca/en/teaching-human-rights-ontario-guide-ontario-schools/appendix-1-glossary-human-rights-terms
Viewed on November 22, 2020

we consciously and unconsciously support the idea of white being supreme.

There are three childhood experiences that stand out for me: one with friends, one with family, and one coping mechanism meant to protect me from the ignorance of strangers. I share them here to illustrate how racism is embedded in the fabric of our societies. The myth of "race" has been so tightly and successfully woven that, even despite family bonds, words create gaps that surreptitiously put us in our place, on the other side.

Ape (What my Friends Taught me about Systemic Racism)

It's a seminal moment
when you get to have a birthday party
and invite your friends from school

Friends…

But the poster they chose
to give me
felt otherwise

I don't remember what it said
I just remember the big ape
that took up all the space
on the paper

And took the air
out of my lungs

Why this poster?

Something inside me suggested I knew

I can still remember the hollow feeling in my stomach when I rolled open the poster. I remember where I was sitting on the back (enclosed) porch of my home on Montreal's West Island. I remember where the givers of the poster were sitting and, interestingly, their smiles and how they looked at each other as I opened it. I also remember never feeling sure if we were friends. Why I invited them to my party is a mystery that now shows up daily in my life as a mother; the way friendships among young girls feel tentative, the ground underneath shifting continuously. They are the only guests I remember at the party, and I only remember them because of this gift. I'd like to say I stopped looking for their acceptance after that. But it's more likely that I did not. I also would love to say that I talked about this feeling that was snaking through my body as I looked at the poster with my parents. I did not. We didn't talk about "race" or racism until I was a teenager, and then it was fleeting. My parents had different entry points; my dad lived it, and my mom couldn't see the subtleties of it. In my home, that meant we didn't talk about it.

I also didn't talk about it with my two friends who were "biracial", my one friend who was brown, or my one friend who was black. I don't think I had the words for it then, and I'm not sure I could have put my finger on the feeling. Now, I can name it as racism, microaggression, exclusion, othering. But at nine, it was confusing and painful, and I simply smiled, said thank you, and never hung up the poster.

Either/or in my life meant I was immersed in one culture and not the other; I had a sense of identity in my European roots and not in my Caribbean roots. If you walked through my childhood home, there would have been little cultural evidence of my dad's presence. That lack shows up in the person I am as well.

When I look back on my life, I wonder: if I had a stronger sense of identity from both "sides," or if we talked more as a family, would I have had the courage and fortitude to *not need* the approval and friendship of those two girls who thought it was funny to give me that poster? I wonder how those things may have changed the trajectory of my life. I recently watched *The Hate U Give*, and my heart ached at the way pride about who they were as people who are black was instilled into the two children by their father.

Logistics of time (my father worked 9–5 as a corporate controller and also taught night school when I was a child), experience (my father grew up in Jamaica, surrounded by people—and people in power—who looked like him), and, maybe, my personality meant I didn't (in my memory) get more than a hallway talk.

Work Harder (The Reality of Being Black in a White World)

"Work harder,"
My dad said to me
when I was eight

A quick, urgent appeal
in the hallway
probably about my homework
but it felt bigger

On one knee
with his hands on my shoulders
eye to eye

"You have to work harder
than everyone else."

A quick hug

I knew what he meant
without more words

I nodded
and took it seriously

Somehow, I knew
that my life depended on it

Despite corporate commitments to diversity and inclusion...

Despite teacher education about isms and the impact of low expectations...

Despite an awareness that not being representative of the population is a mark against a business...

Despite movement to increase diversity (which I believe is window dressing and does little unless the organizational culture becomes inclusive and aware)...

Despite our current climate of heightened awareness of systemic racism...

People with dark skin *still* have to work harder than people with light skin. And even then, recognition isn't guaranteed.

I also consistently hear in client focus groups that the workplace experience can be vastly different—not supportive, not safe, and with different expectations.

Sometimes less is expected—showing up in lack of promotion.

Sometimes more is expected—manifesting in harsher performance reviews or workload or being asked to train someone white to do a job one has been doing already, but not being considered for that position.

Industry doesn't matter in my experience; people who are black experience the workplace and their career trajectory in similar (negative) ways.

Catalyst calls this Emotional Tax:

"Emotional Tax is the heightened experience of being different from peers at work because of your gender and/or race/ethnicity and the associated

*detrimental effects on health, well- being, and the
ability to thrive at work."[14]*

The second memory involves my Oma, who was
definitely racist *and* loved me fiercely.

This is another example of both/and.

Oma was born in Austria in 1911. She lived through
both World Wars in a country that birthed Hitler. She
grew up surrounded by people who were white and was
likely taught about the "savages" who lived in "deepest,
darkest Africa". I can surmise this based on the images in one of the German children's books I read as a
child and the comments she would make about "those"
people (anyone not white). She probably wasn't thrilled
about my mom's choice of husband, and her relationship
with my dad was complicated—as noted in the *"Do You
Like…?"* poem in the previous chapter.

But I have no doubt that my Oma loved me. I spent
most of my time with her in my first years of life. She
likely saw many of my firsts as a result. And because of
that, we had a bond I imagine is typically reserved for
mothers and their daughters.

And, despite all of this, I felt a gap. It seeped into
the space between us, on the coattails of comments and
actions.

---

[14]   https://www.catalyst.org/wp-content/uploads/2019/01/
emotional_tax_how_black_women_and_men_pay_more.pdf
Viewed on November 22, 2020

Noses and Hugs (What my Oma Taught Me about Systemic Racism)

I have images of you
in my memory
that will never fade

Holding open your blankets
in the middle of the night
so I could snuggle with you
when I was scared

Watching you comb your hair
upside down
one brown streak
in waves of grey

Cookies

So many cookies

Playing guitar, dog chases, and singing
soft boiled eggs
in bed
for breakfast

Your smell
how you hugged me
and the sound you made when you did

And...
"You're growing into your nose."

That's there too.
Deep.

I don't know what to do with that one...

It is challenging to remember both of these things at the same time—love and "Othering"—and I can feel my throat getting tighter, even as I write this, suggesting tears are close by. My Oma loved me. And she was taught that all things white were better: the concept of white supremacy. She transferred that to how she saw me. At the time it was hurtful. It meant that somehow, I was not enough. And it came wrapped in a hug and the feeling of comfort, which was confusing.

Microaggressions are often like this. They are insults with a smile. They are backwards compliments. They highlight the colour ladder (as my colleague Dr. Ganz Ferrance calls it); the ordering of value by skin colour with white at the top (the norm, the standard) and all other shades falling underneath in order from lighter to darker. I am sure that even as someone of colour I have unwittingly said or have done something to, or thought something about, someone with darker skin that reinforces this hierarchy. The construct is deeply embedded in our collective psyche. Even in countries predominantly populated by people of colour, you can see evidence of the colour ladder and the concept of white supremacy in who has the "good jobs" and who holds positions of leadership and power.

Microaggressions reinforce the colour ladder and the beliefs of superiority and inferiority that go with it. They also send the message of who belongs and who does not. They get under our skin (no pun intended) and often create discomfort after the fact.

In my experience:

"Oh, you're Canadian?" (read: surprise because you aren't white)

"You *sound* Canadian." (read: if you're not white, you're assumed to be an immigrant and therefore should have an accent)

"Where are you from?" (read: you can't be from Canada, you're not white)

And, sometimes these are seen as positive by those who say them and those who overhear them, which in the absence of an analysis about systemic racism/ anti-black racism makes it challenging to highlight their negative impact. Such as:

"He is so articulate."

"You write so well."

The last childhood memory is one about the ignorance of strangers and my attempt to protect myself from it.

"Mom!" (The Things We Do for Safety)

Shopping
is a carefully constructed plan
on my part

You don't know
the game I play

How when we enter the store
I purposefully distance myself
so I can call to you
and people can hear me say
"Mom"
out loud

I hope it will shelter me
from the eyebrows,
the hiccup of silence,
the quick glances,
when we get to the cash
and reality dawns slowly

You didn't know
didn't see
didn't get it

That makes me sad

And I never told you,
which makes me sad too

Systemic racism/anti-black racism means that we experience the world differently. As a result, we move through the world differently. There are things black people and people of colour need to do for safety, self-preservation, navigation, and access. My example is a small one and about my need (as a child) to have my relationship with my mother recognized. This came back in full force when I decided to have a child of my own, which I will tell you about later.

Other examples of having to navigate the world differently include:

- Watching one's tone so as not to appear aggressive (versus assertive)

- Wondering if you'll be the only person of colour in the room, at the party, in the meeting, etc.

- Changing your name on your CV so you have a better chance of an interview

These considerations and hurdles exist in business, in education, in social circles, in accessing services, etc.

If I were black, I could likely rhyme off many more examples. My light skin and my cultural knowledge mean that I can move through the world with more ease and that many of the hurdles faced by people who are black and people of colour who are darker than me are not on my radar. This is something I teach in my workshops; we see and navigate the world differently based on who we are (skin colour being one facet), and as a result, there are things we will notice and things we will not even know exist.

Systemic racism and the microaggressions that accompany and support it is a "soup" we are all swimming in. We have been born into it, and this means that we can unwittingly—even as people of colour—perpetuate the colour ladder hierarchy.

Either/or allows us to stay on our own "side" if we are white and keeps us on our side if we are black or people of colour. (I have used the words "stay" and "keep" purposefully because social power gives or takes away choice.)

When we begin to see the system of racism/anti-black racism and attune ourselves to the ways our behavior, language, action, and inaction perpetuate it, we can move towards a both/and way of being together and do the work of dismantling it.

Systemic (Anti-Black) Racism at Work

One of the many positive things that have come out of the heightened level of awareness about anti-black racism in the second half of 2020 is the amplification of voices of black people. Because of that, people are stepping forward with programs and initiatives that address lack of representation. One of the challenges with this kind of approach on its own is that diverse representation without an inclusive environment only scratches the surface, and often, people don't stay or don't/can't contribute. Inclusion is the key to diversity, *and it has to come first*. In addition, inclusion without examining and challenging systems of oppression only goes so far.

As my friend and colleague Rodney Patterson[15] (author of *Trumping the Race Card: A National Agenda – Moving Beyond Race and Racism*) says, "What's the point of including someone in an oppressive environment?"

We have to have a three-pronged approach:

1. Cultivating an inclusive environment

2. Creating an environment that is anti-oppressive, which begins and is supported by awareness at the leadership level

3. Increasing diversity

If you are leaning into conversations about "race," here are some questions to ponder.

Questions to Ponder

1. Do you know what systemic anti-black racism looks like in business? What about in *your* company?

2. Are you able to see how anti-black racism creeps into your policies and practices—or their disregard?

---

[15] Rodney Patterson is the principal at The Learners Group, a US-based firm that supports organizational Diversity, Inclusion and Engagement. Rodney Patterson has also written a book called *Trumping the Race Card: A National Agenda – Moving Beyond Race and Racism*
www.thelearnersgroup.com www.trumpingtheracecard.com

3. Do you notice the ways the devaluing of black skin shows up in who is considered, chosen, asked, heard, and taken seriously?

4. Are you able to see how systemic anti-black racism has shaped your company thus far?

CHAPTER 3

Not Black Enough

The lack of awareness and lack of engagement in half of my identity and heritage is not surprising when you consider that my mother (who is white and European) was home with me (and then my brother and me) as we grew up. And my father (who is black and Caribbean) was the sole breadwinner, working a full-time job, and teaching at nights when I was a child.

I gleaned most of my identity from my mother and Oma, the family members with whom I spent the most time as a child. That, and my light skin tone, has afforded me some access to white privilege.

We didn't talk about "race" at home, and I don't remember talking about it with my high school friends who were not white.

There were only a handful of non-white kids at my high school. And the few friends I hung out with at school were a mix: black of Caribbean origins, Chinese, Guyanese, white. The kids I hung out with at the church youth group were mostly white except for one family with three kids.

With the exception of the experiences shared in the last chapter that gave me pause and stirred something inside me that I couldn't quite name, but felt, "race" wasn't something I remember even thinking about.

Two exceptions stand out in high school, but although I was impacted, I still felt removed.

Mom Says You Can't

Almost home

A quick stop to chat
on my schoolfriend's street
finishing our conversation
maybe laughing about the day

"Mom says you're not supposed
to hang out with black people"

Her little sister interrupts

Awkward moments
as my friend
brushes her sister off

But the sentence has landed

She means me

Funny how the only people
who think I'm black
are white...

I remember feeling stunned in this moment. It was my first blatant and overt experience of racism, and it required me to think more about how others saw me. In the Ontario-wide youth group that I participated in through the Presbyterian Church (the Presbyterian Young People's Society – PYPS), I was similarly conspicuous.

Was it a coincidence that the only black guy at PYPS had a crush on me and that some kids were eager to see us together?

Was it a coincidence that I had a crush on the tall blonde guy from my church?

I have always noticed that I have been one of a few people of colour in most situations and spaces I have found myself in. I have always done a count when I arrive in a location. I've only recently considered if this is about curiosity, judging the lay of the land, or just habit. I think it's a bit of all of them. For some people, I imagine it's also about safety.

But not being accepted by the black kids (not being black enough) meant that I didn't consider myself black. This is something that has reared its head in motherhood, which I'll also tell you about later.

That day on the road when my friend's sister interrupted us was my first experience in Canada with overt/blatant racism (that I noticed or remember, besides the inkling about the birthday poster). I was in my teens, which for readers who are black may seem incredulous. But remember, I have light-skin privilege.

This experience created a knot in my stomach and a rush of energy through my body that had me wanting to look her in the eye, to challenge her to address it, at the same time as wanting to keep my eyes down while I wished to disappear. We both stood there, rooted in the moment. The overwhelming feeling I remember was her awkwardness and embarrassment. I knew it was about me, but having never felt black, I felt removed from the comment. It didn't stick. It didn't feel personal beyond a little rush of *she thinks I'm black!*

I don't think I even brought it up at home.

I was used to being different. Remember, my mother is from Austria, and we spent the occasional summer there.

No One Said "Don't Point"

Children point
parents stop and stare
I'm on display
just by being present

An anomaly
a curiosity
a show

Walking through the village
is uncomfortable
even though
being with my family
is home

Let me take you back to Austria in the 1970s. My relatives all lived, and still do for the most part, in small villages. When my mom and I were visiting, traffic would stop. Literally. Children and adults would halt their activities to look at us, at *me*. There was pointing by people of all ages.

I was likely the first non-white individual most of them had ever seen in person. I don't begrudge them for their curiosity. It is similar to how I know that my Oma's bigotry was a product of her surroundings, not her intention.

But it was hard. Or maybe, it's only hard in my memory of it.

Intention doesn't ease impact.

Being seen as different because of my skin colour wasn't new but being called black was.

This labelling didn't change anything for me, however, because I needed it to come from someone who was black for it to matter. Then it would have felt like a rite of passage.

Low Expectations

The next incident that I remember was in my last year of high school. I felt the cold and earth-tilting reality of racism close up.

My favourite subject was English. I loved to read, and I loved to write. No surprise, then, that one of my beloved teachers was the English teacher. I had been fortunate to have been in his class in Grades 9 and 13. His comments on my essays encouraged me. Therefore, I was stunned when I heard him tell my parents at the parent-teacher interview following my participation in the school fashion show that I should pursue a career in modelling. That was a slap in the face, which I can still feel if I close my eyes. I felt passed over, not seen; my writing ability and good grades were discounted in one sentence.

As if modelling was all I should aspire to.

That's how it felt, anyway.

But I digress.

We were asked to do a group project. I jumped on the opportunity to be in a group with Colin—one of only a handful of black guys in our school. Truth be told, I had a crush. He was tall and good looking and had an easy smile. Like all black guys, he was out of my reach. I wasn't white enough, and I wasn't black enough to be anywhere near their world, or so it seemed.

I was invisible.

When Colin agreed to be in the same group as me, I couldn't believe my luck! I felt like I had arrived. I vaguely remember that we were going to turn whatever Shakespeare play we were reading in class into an Arsenio Hall episode.

I thought it was clever. Our teacher did not. In fact, he tried to dissuade me from continuing in the group, making it obvious that he didn't think Colin was a good choice.

I do not remember his words. What I *do* remember is the meeting after class and the sick feeling in my stomach as what he was suggesting sunk in.

I found a place to cry. However, it was not private enough because the social studies teacher found me. I shared my pain and disappointment, and although

I don't remember what she said, I remember that she wasn't surprised.

I wasn't able to look at my English teacher the same way again. I can't tell you how our presentation went or even if we did it. But even then, I realized the uphill battle Colin must have been fighting to be taken seriously (apart from sports, which he played) in that class and likely other classes as well.

I see that same pattern in the organizations I work with. And I now also recognize the incredible toll that it can take—on students of colour and employees of colour alike—not to be taken seriously, to be discounted, to be invisible.

According to the Catalyst report, employees who are black experience "emotional tax" that has them feeling less psychological safety at work, which can lead to a feeling of "being on guard" and to lower rates of contribution. Inclusion can help with this "emotional tax."[16]

Questions to Ponder

One of the things I highlight in my work with clients is the impact of assumptions and how easily we make them and think they are correct. Assumptions can be due to many things, including experience, stereotypes, prejudice, and the messaging of systemic (anti-black) racism that we are bombarded with on a regular basis.

---

[16] https://www.catalyst.org/wp-content/uploads/2019/01/emotional_tax_how_black_women_and_men_pay_more.pdf

1. What assumptions are you making about your employees who are black or people of colour?

2. What has led to those assumptions?

3. What might the impact of those assumptions be on the person in question and on what they may contribute to your team or organization?

CHAPTER 4

Neither—I'm not Black *or* White

By the time I went to university, it felt, looking back, like I had no "racial" identity at all. I was neither black *nor* white.

That's a luxury afforded to me by my light-skinned privilege. If you're white, you don't have to think about "race" because typically we have learned that "race" is about people who aren't white. Robin DiAngelo writes about this in her book, *White Fragility*.

Neither is not the opposite of either/or.

It may feel like a reprieve, but it makes us invisible.

Neither

Neither is an interesting place too.

I mean,
it doesn't really exist,
but I use this to describe
not having a racial identity.

Maybe this is what "not seeing colour"
is like
from the other side.

Nothingness.

I titled this chapter "Neither" because this time in my life was a cultural desert.

I arrived at the University of Guelph campus in the fall of 1989, after what is now called a "gap year." The student population was almost entirely white. Not surprisingly, the basketball team was a notable exception.

I noticed the absence of people of colour, but this wasn't anything new.

I was 19, and I was *used* to being surrounded by people who were white.

I was *used* to being able to count the people of colour in a room on one hand (if at all).

I was *used* to looking different, to standing out.

But I wasn't used to *being* different.

In university, I hit a new demographic.

Not only were *all* of my friends white but also many of them, including a first (and only) boyfriend, were from small towns in Ontario. It's possible, as I think back, that I may have been the first non-white friend for many of them. I was a different kind of different.

Sadly, in an environment meant for broader (and critical) thinking, I still wasn't talking about, exploring, or leaning into "race," not personally and not in classes. A limited but notable exception was a black history course (the first time I *really* learned about the Civil Rights Movement and black history in the USA) and a research trip in the summer before my last year (which I will tell you about later in this chapter).

This new demographic changed me. In some ways, I became a representative of someone black or at least "of colour" for my new friends. That presented a whole range of feelings of inadequacy plus the temptation to try to be someone I was not—relying on limited knowledge and shallow stereotypes.

I started talking about "my white side" and "my black side," mostly in jest. When I missed getting a paper ball into a basket, I joked about my white side. When I busted a move on the dancefloor, I'd joke about my black side. It was a feeble attempt to locate myself and acknowledge my "racial" and cultural shortcomings at the same time.

It provided some levity, but it didn't help me much.

Passing at Work

In the workplace, it's often the people who "aren't too black or too dark-skinned" and who "pass," who are present, and who are allowed (I use that term purposefully) to rise.

What does it mean to "pass"?

In this case it means anyone who is racialized who doesn't remind folks too much about oppression, doesn't ask too many questions, isn't too loud, and is careful about the emotions they show.[17]

It is anyone black who tows the line and doesn't upset the status quo.

Simply put, there are different rules of engagement for people and employees who are black, and many of these are about staying quiet, staying small, not making waves, and making things easier for others (read: for

---

[17] https://www.theatlantic.com/business/archive/2015/10/being-black-work/409990/ Read April 29, 2020

people who are white). This happens at the expense of themselves and their well-being (professional *and* emotional). I have specifically left out people of colour here, because in my experience black people are less represented than people of colour in the workplace. Darker skin makes it harder to pass.

The result is that in order to "make it," people who are black (and people of colour) often try to strip themselves of their culture, of who they are, and assimilate as best they can to fit in. My father did this in the 1960s, 70s, 80s, and 90s. I still see people doing it in companies today. We haven't come as far as we *think* we have despite decades-long conversations about diversity and inclusion.

Brené Brown tells us, in her documentary *The Call to Courage,* that the opposite of belonging is fit. If you have to make yourself fit, it's because you don't belong.

We can't change our skin colour, but people who are black (and people of colour) often strategically attempt to rid themselves of the things that are not "white enough":

- Clothing
- Mannerisms
- Accents
- Names
- Food
- Ways of being

This identity stripping is an attempt to be acknowledged, taken seriously, and have a chance at success.

Think about that for a moment.

What does it feel like to have to be less of who you are to have a chance at success?

Many of you may be able to relate to this in other areas besides "race."

For people who are black in North America, one of the ways this shows up is in school, for instance, when students who are black are told by their peers who are black that they are "acting white" if they are studious and smart.

What is the result?

We have engaged, educated, intelligent, motivated students who are black who have to choose between their "racial" identity and peer group and their dreams for the future.

In the workplace, we have engaged, intelligent, educated, and motivated employees who are black who have to choose to be less of themselves (the criteria for which is largely based on stereotypes) and "act white." What this means is that they feel a pressure to be other than they are—to be things that are *not* associated with being black (thanks to systemic racism) in order to succeed.

My father did that. He made it to the C-Suite. But it came at a price.

University Encounters with "Race"—Part 1
We Don't All Look the Same

Three seminal "race" moments stand out for me during the four years I spent at University. I know, *only* four. Like I said, light-skin privilege and a lack of awareness.

One Colour, Two People

Did she really not notice?
Or was it just speed?
Carelessness?
Or maybe it didn't matter...

Not his name

As if they were interchangeable

Which says a lot about value,
or lack thereof

I didn't really understand
the nuance
to his anger
then

My sociology class lecture hall held about 100 people, maybe more. There were two students in the class who were black and male. One day, the professor mixed up their names as she responded to one of them. Maybe one could excuse her for not knowing all the names in a class of over 100 students. But when there are only two black males, one would imagine that being memorable. And she did know their names. She simply couldn't/didn't tell them apart.

That's another layer of invisibility or indifference.

The reaction of the student she misnamed was powerful.

I don't remember the details of what he said or the professor's response. I *do* recall that her response was inadequate, and the student's analysis was on point. The accusation of racism hung in the air: She couldn't be bothered, or didn't think it necessary, to tell the only two black men in the class apart. And one had glasses! Or maybe it was worse; maybe, she didn't even realize she was doing it.

The professor became more and more flustered and tried, in vain, to justify herself. Her inability to address it, to stand in her privilege, and *own* her racism shook up the class. It was my first experience like this—where someone pointed out racism so clearly—that the experience is etched in my mind. I can still see the lecture hall and where I was sitting in relation to where he was when the exchange took place.

Looking back, I know he took a huge risk. I wonder if that challenge became something the professor took on as a catalyst for personal growth and awareness? I wonder what the cost was to that student?

Being "Colour Blind"

While I'm on the topic of not noticing who someone is...

Sometimes, people who are white think it's better not to notice colour. I think there is a sense that this makes it better and means they can't be racist. But that is because we have all been taught that skin tone has a value attached to it. I believe that people make this leap: When I don't notice your darker skin, it means I'm not devaluing you.

It's that either/or piece again.

In order for me to value you, I have to ignore your colour. I must pretend that I don't see it.

Both/and allows us to see both the skin tone *and* the human being, not the media spin, the stereotypes, and the myths.

Mom Said…

"I don't see your colour,"
you said,
"I love you."

As if these can't
coexist:
being and loving

And I wonder
how you can love <u>me</u>
if you don't see
my brown skin?

When we think not seeing colour is better, what it says to me is that we are saying that being nothing is, in fact, better than being black or brown.

And by the way, how can you not see my skin? It covers all of me. Where are you looking?

Maybe you mean that you don't *want* to notice it because you don't want value to creep in and make me 'less than'?

I figure this is what my mother means; she sees *me*, her child, not what the world suggests she should see when she sees someone with brown skin. I think I get it. But we have to change the paradigm. I can be a person of colour *and* have value. You don't have to strip me of my colour to help me rise in your regard.

"I have a dream that my four little children will one day live in a nation where they will not be judged by the color of their skin but by the content of their character."
– Dr. Martin Luther King, Jr.
I Have a Dream speech, delivered August 28, 1963[18]

Dr. Martin Luther King, Jr. didn't have a dream that suggested we *not see colour* in order to see the content of character.

Colour blindness implies judgment. Otherwise, you wouldn't have to make a point to not notice my skin.

---

[18] Dr. Martin Luther King Jr.'s "I Have a Dream" speech quoted from this website (viewed on August 2, 2020): https://www.americanrhetoric.com/speeches/mlkihaveadream.htm

And not seeing colour can't be the only way you see my value. I believe Dr. King was asking us to lean into both/and.

Who "Makes It"?

Professionals who are black experience another form of neither and invisibility. Look around, and you will notice that it takes a *certain* type of black person to rise in business.

Many people will ascribe that to meritocracy. I ascribe it to learning how to play the game. How far away from being "black" does one have to get to make it in a culture, space, or society built on whiteness? (I added quotation marks around "black" since it's often the *ideas* of blackness—the stereotypes—that people expect.)

What do people who are black have to leave behind in order to rise?

Is it interests, accent, friendship circles, social circles, world view, perspective, experience, pain, dreams, insight, all of the above?

If these aspects match the culture they belong to (in a neighbourhood or workplace), their skin colour becomes only skin. People can overlook it, to a point. Even Barack Obama, as President of the USA, was reminded of his colour, and he made it to the White House!

Which reminds me of my second seminal moment about "race" in university.

University Encounters with "Race"—Part 2 The Gaze

I was enrolled in the Child Studies Program at the University of Guelph. My intention was to become a special education teacher. In my third year, I became interested in assessment and learned about standardized testing and the implications of the structure/content of these tests on kids who weren't white.

At some point, I became interested in what we were then calling inner-city kids (read: kids of colour who live in poverty). The books I was reading were, in my memory, US-based.

Not only did this activate my social justice muscles but it also activated my internalized racism and my white gaze. I wanted to help "those people."

In the summer after my third year, I spent some time in Montreal, visiting my Oma. During that time, I also connected with an incredible human being named Eddie Nurse. Mr. Nurse was a teacher in an "inner-city" high school. I wish I could remember the name of it. It had a large population of students who were black and students of colour. Mr. Nurse was black, and I remember he told me a little about the history of Little Burgundy in Montreal. Little Burgunday was the "black neighbourhood" that sprung up near the train station in the early 1900s and was home to the train porters who were mostly black men[19]. Mr. Nurse had a gift for really seeing his students, and they rewarded that ac-

---

[19]   https://www.thecanadianencyclopedia.ca/en/article/sleeping-car-porters-in-canada

knowledgment by showing up physically in his class and intellectually in their work. I was only in his presence for one afternoon, but I could tell they loved him.

Looking back, Mr. Eddie Nurse was my second *real* introduction to inclusion in action and seeing the bigger picture.[20] My textbooks highlighted the facts—poverty, Eurocentric curriculum and systems, racism (although not named, as I recall). Eddie Nurse's classroom and teaching brought those pages to life. And more than that, he was making a difference. He saw potential. He saw what was possible. He saw the person behind the pain, behind the stereotype. He knew the burden and impact of low expectations and struggle. And he loved those kids—with amazing results.

I was inspired. And, I had an "othering" gaze. I walked into Mr. Nurse's classroom that summer day with my whiteness showing in my lack of awareness of black history in Canada (or at all, for that matter), in my feeling of separateness from his students, in my wanting to "help." Inner city was not my experience, and neither was being black. I'm pretty sure that I came back home excited about what was possible, and I have a

---

[20] My first experience with inclusion in action was through the University of Guelph swimming coach, Alan Fairweather. Al had a policy of accepting anyone onto the team who came to tryouts—putting those of us with less experience/skill on the B team and working with us (should we take up the challenge) at early morning practices until we could join the A team. It's thanks to this policy that I made the A team a few months after tryouts, and made it to the CIAU's for 50 freestyle in my 4th year (and medalled at the Outgames 13 years later, in 2006).

vague memory of wanting to return and do research (I was thinking of applying to a master's degree program). I would use Mr. Nurse's teaching, students, and classroom as my research—to highlight what could be done.

It was an intoxicating opportunity to "do good" and "help," but I had no critical lens with which to assess it or my role, and no awareness or analysis with which to locate myself within that research. And it would seem that my white professors possibly didn't either.

I'm not sure what happened to that dream or the plan to get my master's degree following my undergrad. My fourth year was a blur, and I found myself graduating and starting training as a flight attendant the next day. I did get my master's degree, but not until 8 years later, and with a different focus.

Finally, here is my third experience with "race" in university.

University Encounters with "Race"—Part 3
What Does It Mean to Be Black?

"Oh, Annemarie," one of my new friends said one day. "you're not really black!"

Of course, she was correct. I'm not. I'm mixed.

But that's not what she meant.

She meant that there is nothing—or little—about me besides my melanin that suggested blackness.

What are those stereotypical markers of blackness? A few come to mind:

- Clothing

- Voice/accent

- Language

- How one walks

- Interests

- Music

- Cultural nuance

She was right. I lack all of those stereotypical things. As well as many real markers, like cultural knowledge, gaze, experience, or impact.

I did not have the same cultural immersion into my father's Jamaican heritage as my mother's Austrian heritage. As a consequence, my skin colour, and a few Jamaican dishes, is almost all that I have to suggest my affiliation with Jamaica or any type of blackness.

I also didn't have a black gaze, and I didn't notice that either or know what it meant until a few years ago.

In a world of either/or and white supremacy, we are taught that to "make it", you can't honour who you are if you are not white. You have to pick either success or affiliation. That means organizations that proclaim a diversity and inclusion commitment are mostly window dressing. It's aesthetic and on the surface. We are counting people not making people count.

What I have seen in both corporate and not-for-profits I have worked with over the past 16 years, in terms of numbers, is that black (and even more so Indigenous) people consistently make up the least number of employees. And when they are present, they largely remain in frontline or entry-level positions rather than rising through the organization to positions of leadership.

There are many excuses for that lack of representation and also many practical reasons for it.

Excuses:

- Not qualified
- Not enough experience
- Not the right "fit"
- Seniority
- Not enough diversity in the pipeline

Practical reasons:

- Lack of access and opportunity
- Intersections with poverty as the cycle of oppression is intergenerational, which impacts education, access, and opportunity
- Exhaustion from working in toxic environments
- Turnover, which means no access to seniority
- Racism: meaning, in this case, value and contributions are not seen and concerns are not heard or taken seriously

This last point is what is shifting in this moment in time since George Floyd was killed. People in positions of power (people who are white) are leaning in to listen, consider systemic racism, and hear about its impact. People who are white *want* to know. This will hopefully encourage powerful conversations, and in turn, if people who are white listen and take it in, it can lead to powerful change.

If we had a both/and approach, students who are black wouldn't still be streamed into trades or into sports as entry to post-secondary institutions or as a future. The dropout/pushout[21] rates for students who are black would decrease, and the graduation rates would increase.

We would have more representation in professions like law, medicine, engineering, education, business, and tech—not only because of a more inclusive school experience, or greater awareness about different careers but also because of the possibilities both/and opens up for people to shine, be all of who they are, and be *seen* and *acknowledged* as such.

We would have greater representation of people who are black in positions of leadership and on boards, which is what organizations like *Black North Initiative*[22] are up to. We would have more entrepreneurs who are black.

Here is the crucial piece, however: Representation alone doesn't bring change. Inclusion is the piece we talk

---

[21]   Pushout is a term I have heard in Toronto to explain how black students are pushed out of school by a system and teachers/administrators who don't see them.

[22]   Black North Initiative is Canadian and was founded by Wess Hall in response to the killing of George Floyd and the resulting wave of increased consciousness and leaning into systemic anti-Black racism. www.blacknorth.ca

less about, and the piece that we should be highlighting. Because it's within an environment that acknowledges, values, respects, listens to, and creates space to hear from a diverse representation of employees (and uses those insights and perspectives to *do* things differently) where the benefits of diversity show up.

It's when environments are inclusive, and employees feel a sense of belonging and systemic barriers are removed that companies reap the true benefits of diverse representation. It takes ideas, perspectives, and insights from people who are black and people of colour (and from other Historically Disadvantaged Groups) to create opportunities to make workplaces, products, programs, services, and organizations better for people who are black and for people of colour. In turn, this increases your customer base, improves the experience for clients, and attracts a more diverse staff (including more staff who are black/people of colour).

Plus, your employees who are racialized are more productive, engaged, and present. And they can rise with their identity intact, so their perspectives continue to be shared and inform culture, demographics, and process.

That is inclusion and belonging. That's where we feel the juice. And it comes from both/and:

- Black *and* smart

- Black *and* productive

- Black *and* promotable

- Black *and* leadership material

Both/and requires that we step into the inquiry about "race," its history and racism. And we must remain open to hearing the context not just the story.

It's much more work, but the rewards are great:

- Connection
- Belonging
- More peace
- Love

And in business:

- Productivity
- Engagement
- Customer service
- Market share
- Innovation
- Increased representation (because as people who are black get into leadership, the barriers to promotion will be reduced as racial bias is removed).

Both/And Requires the Truth

Both/and is not meant to brush over and discount our stories and our pain in favour of moving forward. When our stories and our pain are heard and held, we move forward together.

For me, as a brown woman and a brown business owner, I see colour all the time!

I count the people of colour in any room I walk into. I always have.

In my work life, I am often the only person of colour in the room.

And I *know* that I have access: It's because, as my friend accurately pointed out, I'm not really black.

So, I guess white people *do* see colour...

Neither Is a Strange Place

I left high school and my posse of multicultural friends at the age of 18, and I didn't have a non-white friend in my life until I was 23—and then only the one, until I was 31.

The saddest part is that I didn't notice that fact until I took stock and did some reflection in my forties.

I wonder what that did to my spirit? And what my life may have been like otherwise?

Today, I know this;

I'm not white. And I'm not black.

That doesn't make me either/or. It doesn't require that I pick.

It also doesn't make me neither because I don't measure up to either one.

Both of these energies and beliefs have been limiting.

It makes me both/and.

It means I have a certain quantity of melanin, *my* quantity.

It makes me, me.

Because I have my own stories.

But it took me a long time to realize and recognize all of this.

And for a while, I just chose to be neither.

"Neither" is a strange place. On the one hand, it's easy (or easier) than running between either and or, not having a racial identity. Neither means you don't have to prove anything.

But my memories of university feel hollow, like I wasn't really there.

If your work environment isn't inclusive, if your people don't feel like they belong, they won't really be there either. They won't "show up."

And any ROI you thought you were getting because of diversity will be limited.

Questions to Ponder

1. How represented are people who are black and people of colour in your organization? And where is that representation?

2. Would you say that the racial diversity you *do* have in your organization is represented both physically (at all levels) *and* in your policies and practices?

3. If you have employees who are black or people of colour, do you hear from them? If so, when and how?

4. How do you mitigate racial bias in your recruitment, hiring, and promotion process?

CHAPTER 5

On a Mission: Find Some Black Friends

This wasn't a conscious mission, but it happened.

The day after I graduated from University, I started training to be a flight attendant. This was not an industry populated by many people of colour. Not in Canada anyway. As luck would have it, however, I met three of the few employees of colour at the company in my first month on the job. We were all on the same crew, and I struck up a friendship with a "biracial" colleague, Marianna. As it turned out, we discovered that I went to high school with her sister. Marianna's sister and I weren't friends in high school, but we knew each other. I had no idea she was "biracial."

Our "racial" identities didn't figure predominantly in our new friendship. Because Marianna identified as a lesbian and I was starting to question my sexual orientation, we spoke more about that. She was the first person I had found with whom I could talk to about my questions, and not feel ashamed or awkward.

My first trip to Toronto's Gay Village was an unplanned walk east along Wellesley Street from the subway station to Jarvis Collegiate years before. At that time, I had no idea where I was, but I had experienced a strong and inexplicable sense of calm. What I felt when I returned to the neighbourhood with Marianna was no different, except now I knew why. Pride became my new favourite holiday, and I felt a lightness of being—not only because I was accepting who I was but also because I felt I finally had a community to belong to.

That was short-lived.

I subsequently discovered that being bisexual—another refusal to be categorized into a neat box, another example of both/and—wasn't accepted in many LGBTQ2SI+[23] circles despite the prominent placement of the B in the acronym. For me, that meant it was easier to identify as a lesbian when I found myself in relationships with women. But just like the ping-pong experience with "race," it complicated my journey and made it difficult for me to fully step into who I am.

For better or worse, the LGBTQ2SI+ community is where I landed, and I was happy to have a touchstone of some kind. It became "the world I lived in" and is where I have met and made most of my friends, acquaintances, and business contacts since coming out at the age of 27. Many of these people are black or people of colour. Although it is tempting to believe that experiences of oppression and marginalization mean we are more open and inclusive toward others, it is important to note that racism is experienced by people who are black, Indigenous, and people of colour (BIPOC) in LGBTQ2SI+ communities

---

[23] LGBTQ2SI+ stands for Lesbian, Gay, Bisexual, Transgender, Queer/Questioning, Two Spirit, Intersex and the + represents the wide array of sexual and gender diversities

as well. And homophobia, biphobia, and transphobia are also experienced by BIPOC individuals who identify as LGBTQ2SI+ in their cultural communities.

At the age of 31, after leaving the airlines to be a teacher and after teaching for five years and leaving that, I embarked on a new journey—writing. I joined *Siren Magazine* as a writer. At that time, *Siren* was a free, volunteer-run, monthly, lesbian publication. In time, I became the managing editor. I loved everything about it; however, sustaining the magazine became increasingly difficult. It amazed me how much more of a challenge it was to sell advertising for a women's publication when the gay men's magazines were flourishing. After 19 years, *Siren Magazine* printed its last issue in 2004.

Siren gave me a place in the community, and through it, I made two new friends.

Susan and I met at a literary event on Church Street (*the* street in Toronto's Gay Village). Fireweed (a journal) was launching its "biracial" issue. Susan and I happened to be sitting next to each other. The theme lent itself to striking up a conversation about being "biracial."

Tans (We are Not the Same, and That's Okay)

"Don't compare your tan to mine,"
she says with disdain

We are at a magazine launch

Fireweed
The "biracial" issue

We have just met.
She is beautiful,
lighter skinned than me
but definitely not white
Indian and Scottish
as it turns out

We are sharing stories

I remember my Oma's arm
next to mine
as Susan tells me her experience
of comparing skin tones

It's the first time
I have considered
the impact of my Oma's words

The first time I have been
introduced to them
through "racial" eyes

I have to catch up

I nod in agreement
because she is so angry about it
and I'm supposed to be too

I go home that night
feeling less black

again

Our first meeting left me with a lot to think about, but I knew I had found a friend. Susan brought an analysis and a "racial" awareness to my life that was new and made me think. We have had many conversations about "race" over the 20 years since we met. Our common bond of being "biracial" (or "multiracial" in her case if you go back one more generation) has allowed me to open up, explore, and share my feelings and struggle around not being black enough. Our friendship has been a safe space to ask questions, dig deeper, and unravel my experiences, understanding, and (mis)perceptions.

Our common mixed identity is a constant source of amusement as we share stories of people asking us where we are from, what we are, and making assumptions about what we know and don't know. With the availability of genetic testing through 23 and Me, we have laughed about the reality that although my skin is a bit darker than hers, she likely has more people of colour in her family tree than I do. Susan and I have the freedom and permission to explore, ask questions, and joke about our melanin because we have similar experiences of not being identifiable, not being recognized, and not being accepted. In addition to her more melanin-rich ancestry, Susan grew up in a Toronto neighbourhood with a predominantly black population. So, despite her not having (recent) African or Caribbean roots, she has more Caribbean cultural knowledge than I do. It's ironic that despite her lighter skin, she is more black than I am.

I met Laurie at a *Siren* meeting, and we quickly discovered that we had been at the University of Guelph together. She played basketball and had seen me at the

University Athletic Centre. I was embarrassed to admit I had no recollection of seeing her. In addition to being shy, I had two singular focuses in university: grades and swimming. There was little time for gazing around or entertaining the idea of a chat as I made my way down the long Athletic Centre hallway adjacent to the gym, which was lined with photographs of past athletes (mostly white), on my way to or from the pool.

Plus, truth be told, given my sense of not feeling black enough, I think I would have felt awkward and conspicuous had she approached me at university. As it was, I was a little in awe that we were speaking and felt like I had won the lottery when it became clear that we were becoming friends. I couldn't believe it! I did several "happy dances" after our first talks or meetings. We both loved writing and were on our coming out journeys; there was much to talk about.

And, I felt a gap between us that was hard to cross because I still didn't feel black enough.

My First Black Friend in Years

We are both writers
we laugh together
she tells me we were at U of G
at the same time

I didn't notice

Typical

Her friendship
reminds me
again
of who I am not,
who I wish I was

It also invites me in
to a world
I have longed
to be part of
even if just a little
since the Bus Stop

There are demons there
of course

Invited,
I'm in a room
with women of colour
but not really there

Scared to be revealed

seen
to give them proof
of the light skin I carry

As if they didn't already know
or would be surprised

I add the little bits
I can
that I feel legitimize my presence

Some experience
some knowing

having listened closely all these years
I know where to laugh

It's not a place that is mine

I'm a guest
but I want so much
to be allowed
to stay

I continued to meet many other amazing friends and colleagues through the LGBTQ2SI+ community, many of them BIPOC. My world and my life expanded as I created my business, embraced my sexual identity, and became more connected to who I am. Because of my work, I lived in the world of anti-racism, anti-oppression, and diversity and inclusion, and I began to settle into my "racial" identity a bit more. I started calling myself "brown." I liked it because it felt like it accurately spoke to who I am. Later, I would come to realize that it was a term South Asian people used, which complicated things for me (although rumour has it that my paternal great-grandmother was from India).

Acceptance...?

When I was 38, I met Shani.

We met at a party of a mutual friend and hit it off. We discovered we were neighbours and shared a taxi home. After a few phone calls and text messages, we went on our first date. Shani is Caribbean and came to Canada as a university student. I was pleasantly surprised by the ease that I felt in her presence. I remember thinking that maybe I had "arrived." Maybe through the trajectory of new friendships with people who are black and people of colour and my work and personal work, I was somehow black enough to be seen as "dating material" by a Caribbean woman.

I Can Cut a Pineapple (Stereotypes and Other Things that Bind Us)

My new girlfriend is black!

Not only that
she is from
the Caribbean

My dad will be so pleased

and maybe I will
get some "black points"

My street cred
goes up
when I cut
a pineapple for her
the first time

"Whoa!
You are Caribbean!"
she says to me
and I beam

There is something I know
about being black
after all

A little part of me is dancing

It's just a pineapple
but still...

Maybe there is hope

What occurred, as a result of this relationship, is another link to the Caribbean and a prominent black lens and gaze in my life. I also found someone with whom I was able to be myself, and she accepted me completely with all the things I knew and didn't know. She was also someone with whom I could talk about my work. When we met, I had been a diversity and inclusion facilitator and consultant for five years. Shani reminded me about the different experiences and lenses of people who are black who are immigrants to Canada, compared to those who are born in Canada.

This awareness germinated in a work experience a few years earlier where I met another dear friend. Vicki is also an Anti-Racism/Anti-Oppression (ARAO) and D&I facilitator and consultant, and also "biracial" (although black-presenting). Our friendship grew on our commute by GO bus from Toronto to the city of Hamilton to participate in an anti-racism pilot training as facilitators. During that engagement, we heard from a woman who had immigrated to Canada from the Democratic Republic of the Congo. She shared how painful it was for her to raise her son here in Canada, as a black boy. She grieved the richness he was missing, not being surrounded by examples of people in power who looked like him (as she had been growing up). It was something she couldn't have anticipated the impact or significance of before she came.

Think about the implications of growing up in a country surrounded by people who look like you. In North America, this isn't challenging if you are white or if you are a person who is black or a person of colour who has immigrated as an adult from a country in which you were the majority. But if you are a person who is black or a person of colour born in North America, this may be a stretch.

That immersion provides role models and self-esteem, which creates a different flavor of resistance and resilience. I see evidence of it in my father's outlook and stories as well.

I remember the first time I went to Caribana.[24] I was a teenager, and we were living in Mississauga. The parade was on Toronto's University Avenue then. I remember coming up out of the Osgoode Subway station, on the north east side of Queen St. and University St., and being awestruck by the sea of black people as far as I could see. I had been to Jamaica several times by then, but there was something impressive about that image and experience at home that has stayed with me. If I close my eyes, I can still see and feel it; the wonder. There was an almost imperceptible relaxation that I felt in my body. I remember smiling and standing for a moment at the top of the stairs to take it in before joining the crowd.

So, if you are a person who is black or a person of colour who was born in Canada or the USA (or any other majority-white country), I invite you to consider the implications of growing up in a country surrounded by people who look like you and what this means for how children imagine their future and the possibilities it holds for them.

---

[24]   Caribana—now called the Scotiabank Caribbean Festival—takes place in Toronto on the first weekend in August, and is the largest Caribbean festival outside of the Caribbean.

I have heard many African people—famous and not—say how they didn't realize they were black until they arrived in North America.

Hold on.

Before you fly back to the section on Colour Blindness, that's not what I'm talking about here.

When you live in a space where everyone's skin colour is not white, melanin ceases to be a qualifier. In countries populated by people who are black, people are simply people. We find other ways of categorizing, of course, including skin tone or shades of colour, thanks to the globally pervasive concept of white supremacy. But when you grow up with role models of all kinds, and in all areas of life, who look like you, it shows you what is possible. Someone who looks like you allows you to dream that maybe you could aspire to that same position. It's one of the reasons why Barack Obama's US presidency was so groundbreaking; children who are black could finally imagine themselves and dream of becoming the president of the United States of America or the first lady. Because someone who looks like them already had. The same will happen for girls who are black or of colour now that we will have a US vice president who is a woman of colour, and a black woman as the leader of Canada's Green Party. And it will be another step when there is a president of the United States of America or a prime minister of Canada who is a person of colour.

I believe that "racial" immersion (being surrounded by people who look like you) supports the human spirit. It's why systemic racism and the ensuing lack of repre-sentation of people who are black and people of colour in positions of leadership across professions is so dev-astating to children who are black and brown and their images of what is possible—for themselves and for oth-ers. Lack of representation impacts *all* kids. For kids who are black and of colour, it means a lack of folks to model themselves after and hold as possibilities, and possibly a lack of awareness of careers to aspire to. It impacts the futures they see for themselves. Role models are mirrors of possibility. For kids who are white, lack of representation of people who are black and people of colour means they don't see people who are black or people of colour in leadership roles and in a variety of careers. This reinforces stereotypes and prejudice and the erroneous belief that leaders and professionals are not/cannot be black or people of colour. Both impacts are damaging to our collective growth and health and to our connection as people and as societies.

Representation of people who are black and people of colour at all levels is not only important for those we represent but also to help break the myths and stereo-types that (along with other aspects of systemic racism) keep people who are black and people of colour out—out of careers, professions, positions, promotions, and leadership roles.

In the USA, African Americans make up 13% of the population, and in 2018, "held just 3.3% of all executive or senior leadership roles, which are defined as within two reporting levels of the CEO, according to the US Equal Employment Opportunity Commission."[25]

---

[25]   https://www.cnn.com/2020/06/02/success/diversi-ty-and-black-leadership-in-corporate-america/index.html

Lack of Representation in the Workplace

If I asked you to close your eyes and think of a CEO, what picture (or actual person) would come to mind?

Try it and see.

When I do this in workshops or presentations and then ask for a show of hands, the majority of hands raised indicate that people visualize CEOs as white and male (and tall, able-bodied, and with hair). There is a good reason for this; almost all CEOs of Fortune 500 companies today fit at least the first two descriptors on that list.

According to *Fortune Magazine*, "Among Fortune 500 companies, less than 1% of CEOs are black. Today there are only 4, down from a high of 6 in 2012, according to Fortune. And over the past two decades, there have only been 17 black CEOs in total. Of those, only one has been a woman -- Ursula Burns, who ran Xerox from 2009 to 2016. But among Fortune 100 companies this year, black professionals account for just 3% of CEOs."[26]

In the wake of the killing of George Floyd in Minneapolis, USA on May 25, 2020, and the ensuing worldwide protests, I have received many calls from companies asking for help with their D&I efforts. In almost every conversation, the leadership has said something that acknowledges that the people on their

---

Viewed on September 13, 2020

[26]   https://www.cnn.com/2020/06/02/success/diversity-and-black-leadership-in-corporate-america/index.html
Viewed on September 13, 2020

leadership team are mostly (or all) white. And mostly, they are men.

This is not new.

What *is* new is that people are noticing and recognizing it, what it suggests, and that it's a problem.

Lack of representation of people who are black and people of colour is a symptom of systemic racism and systemic anti-black racism. We can trace it back through history and into individual people's lives as early as birth when unconscious bias begins its insidious trajectory; fueling expectations and how they are seen, perceived, and treated, and ultimately (as a result) impacting self-esteem and their success.

The impact of lack of representation in the business world is consistent with the impact in education and in other careers. We see most people who are black and people of colour in entry-level positions and, to a lesser extent, management positions. When we look higher in the business world hierarchy, diversity disappears. Who we find among VPs, Directors, C-Suite, and around the board of directors tables are mostly still white men.

Lack of representation breeds the same if we are not aware of the systems that support it, and if we don't dismantle those systems. The reason is simple; who we see in leadership roles over time becomes who we expect to see. The flip side is also true; those we rarely or never see in leadership roles over time become those we don't expect to see; *those we don't think can be in those roles.* The impact of this is devastating to under-represented communities because this belief is often absorbed, because of a lack of role models *and* because of the bias that then lives in the minds of those in power, and that impacts and informs choices around hiring, mentorship, promotion, and, in the case of boards and politicians, who we elect. It also impacts how the few people who are black and people of colour who *do* make it through to the "top" are seen, heard, treated, and accepted in their leadership roles.

Over the years in Canada and the USA, we have seen a push for increased representation in boards of directors. The Canadian Board Diversity Council (CBCD) was founded in 2010 and reports on board diversity progress. "The 2018 Annual Report Card (ARC)[27] reveals that Canadian boards and C-suites are increasing their representation and diversity at a borderline-stagnant pace." While the CBDC does report on visible minority representation, most of the focus in their annual report is on women where (not surprisingly) the most progress has been made over the years. In addition, visible minorities are all grouped together, meaning we don't have a number specifically for representation of people who are black. My hunch is that those numbers are extremely low. Furthermore, we don't know how visible minority intersects with gender in this data. Generally speaking, however, given systemic racism/anti-black racism, advancements in gender diversity have benefitted women who are white.

---

[27]   https://cdn.ymaws.com/wxnetwork.com/resource/resmgr/images/diversity_council/arc_report_2018_-_pdf/arc_-_annual_report_card_201.pdf Sourced: December 30, 2020.

In June 2020, the Black North Initiative[28] was founded with the intention to increase the representation of Black professionals in the C-Suite and on boards. Hundreds of Canadian companies have signed on to this pledge, which is amazing. It speaks to an awareness (or a desire to be seen as aware) that lack of representation is a problem. I hope it means there are some meaningful conversations happening in those teams and around those tables as a result.

There *is* hope because the beauty of the time we find ourselves in as I wrote this (in the summer and fall of 2020) is that people are now listening differently and talking about a lack of representation in the context of systemic racism. I hope those conversations continue and deepen.

Pressure for increased representation has the potential for change, but it can be surface change, which can be dangerous. When we increase representation without also examining the environment, we have the potential for trouble.

Increasing the representation of people who are black and people of colour

- without the awareness of how systemic racism and systemic anti-black racism manifests in the workplace, in professional environments, in all levels of education, in the trajectory of people's lives;

- without creating an inclusive environment where all are seen, heard, and valued;

---

[28]   https://www.blacknorth.ca/Home Sourced: September 6, 2020

- without addressing systemic racism and systemic anti-black racism in policies and practices;

- without understanding microaggressions and creating an environment where they are addressed and not accepted; and

- without creating a culture that is safer, where people can learn, and where there is a sense of belonging for everyone,

may result in your organization *looking* different, but people either won't be able to really show up or they won't stay. This means that you may return to a lack of representation, or you will have a visibly diverse workforce without the accompanying benefits of increased engagement, productivity, innovation, and creativity.

It's not just about who is there.

It's about creating an environment that allows for sharing of diverse perspectives and insights, people being taken seriously, being seen, heard, and valued, and having that environment change as a result of increased awareness, education, growth, and representation. An inclusive environment where systemic racism and systemic anti-black racism are being addressed and mitigated allows for diversity of thought, innovation, and creativity that is taken seriously and that changes an organization for the better—creating a healthier and continuously more diverse workplace community that attracts and retains more diverse employees *and* serves a broader representation of customers and clients *well*.

It's not just about who is around the table (diversity); it's about who is seen, heard, and valued around that table (inclusion).

The bottom line? Increasing representation of people who are black and people of colour without education, awareness, and addressing systemic racism/systemic anti-black racism in policy and practice is hollow and feels like a "good show," but without substance, it offers little return on your investment.

Questions to Ponder

1. Do you know what systemic anti-black racism looks like in business? In *your* company?

2. Are you able to see how it creeps into your policies and practices—or their disregard?

3. Do you notice the ways the devaluing of black skin shows up in who is considered, chosen, asked, heard, and taken seriously?

4. Are you able to see how systemic anti-black racism has shaped your company thus far?

CHAPTER 6

I Don't Want to Have to Prove that I'm My Daughter's Mother (We Still Group People by Skin Colour)

Speaking of representation, let's fast-forward about six years in my timeline.

Although I knew at the age of 31 that I wanted to be a mother, it took me 12 years to get there.

One of the main issues initially was due to another either/or dynamic; I couldn't figure out how to have a family as a queer-identified[29] woman.

That may sound silly today, but in the early 2000s, there were few role models. Being LGBTQ2SI+ was not as "mainstream" as it is now, in some parts of North

---

[29] Queer is a word that used to be a derogatory term used against people who are gay or lesbian or bisexual. It is still used this way in some places in Canada, the USA and around the world. But it is also now a word that is "reclaimed"—used by some (not all) members of 2SLGBTQI+ communities as a source of pride. It's an umbrella term that encompasses all the letters in the acronym, which is why I like to use it. It lends a bit of anonymity within the label.

America.[30] We didn't have TV shows like *Modern Family*. Plus, until I was 23, I had never *met* anyone who identified as LGBTQ2SI+ (that I knew of).

Because I had grown up in a nuclear, heteronormative[31] family and was surrounded by those images in media, books, and community, that was my internal map of "family." Given I was more attracted to, and therefore in relationships with, women, I felt lost for how to become a mother outside of that heteronormative paradigm.

It sounds incredible to me now, looking back, but at the time, it was a source of incredible pain, confusion, and discomfort. And I made a few decisions and took a few turns that I regret because I hurt people in the process of trying to reconcile my identity and my dream. This is another example of how important it is to have role models—people who show us what is possible because they are *like us* in some way (gender/gender identity, skin colour, sexual orientation, ability, etc.).

In the end, at the age of 36, I decided that I was going to have a child, and I would do it as a single parent. I figured if my Oma could do it in post-war Austria in 1939, I could do it in 2006. I had done a lot of unlearning in the previous four and a half years about what family looks like and means, about the expectations I had of myself, and learning to be true to who I was. I had made peace with not having a heteronormative nuclear family or a partner (of either gender).

One thing I couldn't put aside was the desire for my child to know the other half of their genetic makeup.

---

[30] ILGA stats globally

[31] Explain heteronormative

Maybe this is a result of seeing my mom's pain about not knowing her father (he was killed in WWII when she was three years old), but I couldn't shake it. What this meant for me was that I wasn't going to be searching through profiles in a sperm bank. I was going to have to find a man who would agree to be a known sperm donor. I found hardly any role models for this. Although I had met a few queer women in Toronto who had done the former and would eventually take a course called *Dykes Planning Tykes* to help plan and consider options, there were much fewer examples of queer women with known donors. I had no idea how I was going to do it, but I figured my best chance of finding a known donor would be to look in the gay community.

Besides my certainty about finding a known donor, I was also certain that I wanted to find a man of colour, because I knew for sure that I wanted a child who looked like me.

I Want a Brown Baby (Because We Do See Colour!)

I want a brown baby

I am very clear about that
although I am careful
not to speak about it too much.

Given my work in D&I,
I feel awkward saying it out loud
after all, colour shouldn't matter

Except it does

My parents do not understand this desire

"As long as the baby is healthy" is what they say
when I express it
And of course, they are right

But then what do they know about lack of belonging?
Rooted as they are in their cultures
and countries of origin
that would claim them,
and that they call home?

I want a brown baby
And here's why:

I want a child who looks like me
Who people recognize on sight as mine
I don't want to be asked,
like my mother was,

If I'm babysitting,
if I'm the nanny
I don't want to have to explain whose mother I am
at parent–teacher interviews.

No raised eyebrows or mental math

I had enough of that as a kid
I don't want to replicate the experience

That was the 1970s
And things are different
Things should be different…

But eyebrows don't lie

This certainty about finding a man of colour gave me pause. It was a source of shame; as someone who teaches and speaks about diversity and inclusion, shouldn't this not matter? In many ways, I understood what my parents were saying. But as a "biracial" person, I wanted to have a child who people would recognize as mine because we *do* see colour, whether we claim to or not. I did not want a repeat of my childhood experiences; I did not want to have to explain who I was. (By the way, this confusion never happened when I was with my father. I suppose that our brown skin, although different shades, made it possible for people to make the connection that they couldn't make with my mother and me.)

It took me three and a half years to find a known donor.

Best Laid Plans (The Way the Myth of "Race" Ties Us Up in Knots)

I am planning
the best father,
the best skin colour
for you

As if I know
what you will need

What your hopes are
or will be

Where your life
will take you

Or what will help you
to "pass"
give you less trouble,
make you (in) visible,
depending on the danger

Perhaps
these decisions
are not for you at all
but my demons

The "not enough"
that will keep me searching
until it's too late
to find you

From the age of 36 to just over 39, I met with and spoke with 13 men in my search for a known sperm donor. Some conversations were short and ended there; some took much longer and were more involved. As time moved on, I became more focused on finding a donor who was black, not just a person of colour. I was surprised and delighted by the pull of the familiar with the men I talked with who were born in the Caribbean; it made me happy to feel some affinity.

In the end, I found Benjamin: a man who is black, with Caribbean parents.

Eventually, I gave birth to a daughter.

And then, I began to realize I had missed something.

I Have a Brown Baby

I wanted a brown baby

One that people would recognize
as mine

I learned that the universe
listens carefully
as my child is born not only
with skin the same shade as mine,
but also looks like me

The three words I used most often
when explaining my desire

But here's what I didn't consider
in my choosing:
that my feelings of
inadequacy
would haunt me here, too,
in motherhood

I cannot do cornrows.
I allow my child to run free with "crazy hair"
I am aware of the judging gaze
of black women
whose children's hair
is always neat
It has to be

I am not black enough
Again

Diversity Is about More Than Skin Colour, but Colour Matters

Black is not just a colour. Being black is not just about skin colour. It's a way of being; it's a way of seeing and experiencing the world.

The Black Diaspora is a diverse group, but skin colour has history, and it is one of the things that informs who we are. In a world shaped by white supremacy and systemic racism/systemic anti-black racism, skin colour also affects how we move through the world and how we are perceived and treated.

Often what I see in organizations is the desire for diversity without the accompanying "messiness" that comes with difference.

In my experience, organizations see diversity as a goal without realizing that the human component means we bring perspectives, ideas, experiences, insights, and pain to the table with us. I see this even more so when it comes to "race."

This surface interaction with diversity presents a significant challenge to diversity and inclusion efforts in companies and organizations – or *anywhere*, for that matter.

Over the past decades, we have seen a surge in awareness about diversity (the lack thereof, the need for representation) without a similar awareness of the need for inclusion. The leaning in that happened in the summer of 2020 is no different; organizations and conversations are focusing on the lack of representation of people who are black, particularly in leadership. These are important conversations but fall short if we don't also look at inclusion.

Inclusion would allow the people who arrive in organizations and companies to be seen, heard, and valued *for who they are, and with an awareness of what that means*. Instead, we want to keep the status quo and invite people who *look different* to join us but not *be different* or *make a difference* or *inspire difference* once they are there.

The danger here is that we ask people who are black and people of colour to step into a climate that doesn't see them, won't *want* to see them, and won't know what to *do* with them or their ideas when they are there and have insights and perspectives to contribute.

For many people who are black or people of colour, this means that they will make a choice to keep their job by keeping quiet, staying small, and forgetting a part of themselves. Or they will choose to leave. Or they will be asked to leave because the impact of lack of inclusion is mistakenly seen as a flaw *in them*.

People of colour and people who are black who are born in North America have already experienced this dance through their lifetime in school, and so when they arrive in the workplace, they may already be adept at this hiding, this denying of who they are to succeed in a world that doesn't want to see them. We call this "code switching". But people of colour, and people who are black who arrive in North America as adult immigrants, have to *learn* this dance. Remember the woman

I mentioned who was from the Democratic Republic of the Congo and who spoke about what her son is missing[32]?

Either way, the dance is soul destroying for the individuals and shortsighted for companies and organizations as they miss the opportunity to see more, be more, and go further—both internally in terms of employee engagement, productivity, and satisfaction, as well as externally with customer service, reaching new markets, and product development.

This aesthetic diversity without substance is evident to those it impacts. As a leader, becoming aware of this impact will make a significant difference in how, and who, you lead.

Questions to Ponder

1. Do you know who your employees are? Do you collect demographic data?

2. Do you do regular employee engagement/D&I surveys that include demographic data? How will you know how you are doing if you don't know who is there and how they feel?

3. What does your leadership team look like? Even just visually, whose voices and experiences are missing from those tables?

4. What is the impact? What are you *missing*? What are the implications of question #3 in

---

[32] See the Acceptance...? section in Chapter 5 for the story.

terms of voice, input, leadership, and ultimately your ROI?

The Benefits of "People Like You"

When I met these new friends who are black and people of colour in my early 30s, I realized what I had been missing.

It was nothing I could put my finger on, but it was there: a subtle relaxation that I hadn't felt in years around a friend. When you are with people "like you," there are things you don't have to explain. This is also my experience with people who are part of LGBTQ2SI+ communities; we have some similar experiences, and that creates a knowing and an ease.

Due to my heritage, I could also say that people who are white are "like me." There are some things I just "get," and I understand the "white world" to some extent. But my skin colour undermines some of that knowing and comfort.

Robin DiAngelo ends one of her videos with a profound statement that gave me pause. She says that up to a certain point in her life, she had been able to be in completely white spaces, surrounded by white people, and have white mentors and white leadership—and here is the kicker— *without anyone ever suggesting that there was a loss in that.*

When I heard this, I cried. Because with a few exceptions, that was my life too. And not only did no one have that talk with me, but also I didn't notice the loss myself.

I felt it—in retrospect—when I started to expand my circle of friends in my 30s, and I have felt it growing ever since. Understanding that loss has been painful.

As human beings, we gravitate to people who are like us, who we have things in common with.

In fact, research shows that we "lean in" to people we even *think* we have something in common with. Skin colour and culture are large and (often) visible common denominators.

Consider your team. Who have you hired? How are they "like you"? What made you "lean in"?

When you are the odd one out, you have no choice but to hang out with those who are not like you. But if you have a choice, guaranteed you will look for the person who looks like you or is like you in some way.

Skin colour is an easy pick. You can spot it from a distance. I count the people of colour the minute I walk into a room. Often at business or entrepreneurial events, there are few of us. Very often, in meetings, I'm the only one. I have to find some other reason to "lean in."

In the workplace, we are asking people to be inclusive, to create community, and foster a sense of belonging. That doesn't mean we shouldn't be sitting with people "like us" at lunch or cultivating friendships with people "like us."

I think it's fair to say that the more we have in common, the more comfortable we feel. Skin colour and culture are among the identity markers that we choose to make those initial decisions. (Religion, sexual orientation, income level, and family status are others, but we don't find out about those as quickly.)

The Value of Three

In D&I, the magic number is often three.[33] If you have three or more people with a common identity (gender, skin colour, age, religion, sexual orientation, etc.) then the "value" of diversity *begins* to show up (if, and only if, your space is inclusive, meaning that people feel a sense of safety and belonging). One alone may be too risky to speak up; two we can easily polarize and discount both opinions if they disagree, but three...three is the balancer. Things start to get more real.

Of course, critical mass is important to create change. It signals a need or makes that need more evident. Numbers (in the right environment) can amplify voices and needs, so when there are more people of a certain identity, we not only notice them more but also have more reason to pay attention.

Take the tech industry, for example. Gender diversity has been the focus for many years, with good reason. But people who are black continue to be underrepresented. For example, Google published their numbers in 2014, and only 1.9% of their 5000 employees were black. In 2018, despite diversity efforts to the tune of

---

[33]   https://www.nysscpa.org/news/publications/nextgen/nextgen-article/study-when-it-comes-to-women-on-corporate-boards-three-is-the-magic-number-121218 (accessed April 29, 2020). Also mentioned in the CBDC Annual Report https://cdn.ymaws.com/wxnetwork.com/resource/resmgr/images/diversity council/arc report 2018 - pdf/arc - annual report card 201.pdf (accessed December 30, 2020).

$150 million, the number had only crept up to 3.7%. (African Americans make up 8.6% of tech graduates.)[34]

Until there are more employees who are black in tech (for example), the needs and realities of those employees won't be on the industry radar. And the few black employees that are present will likely keep their heads down and get their work done to keep their job.

And while we are on the topic of gender, what about women who are black? Recognizing the intersection of identities within D&I is not something we do well. Consider all of the work we have done for gender equality in the workplace. Looking at representation on boards and in leadership (just like we are doing now for people who are black), how are we "moving the dial" on women in tech? What you will see if you look closely is that the women who benefit from these efforts (in tech and elsewhere) are mostly white.

Not one of us is only one thing, and the impacts of "race" *and* gender are not just twofold. They are exponential. When we talk about diversity, when we talk about "race" and creating spaces where people belong, we have to remember that our needs and realities (and perspectives and insights) are related to and compounded by *all* of our identities.

But back to the things we have in common.

---

[34] https://www.latimes.com/business/technology/story/2020-06-24/tech-started-publicly-taking-lack-of-diversity-seriously-in-2014-why-has-so-little-changed-for-black-workers (accessed September 13, 2020).

Employee Resource Groups (ERGs)

ERGs exist in 90% of Fortune 500 companies, and 8.5% of Americans belong to an ERG (4.5% of folks in other countries).[35] Although some may find ERGs counterintuitive and undermining of inclusion efforts, those identity-specific spaces are *crucial* for sharing, support, and surfacing issues that organizations must confront and tackle head-on if they want to do the real work of diversity and inclusion. ERGs are more than a social club. When used correctly, they can serve an important purpose of providing a safer space and the opportunity to support their members while educating others and contributing to the creation of more inclusive workplaces in policy and practice.

ERGs for employees who are black have an opportunity to help navigate the conversation about "race." But this will only happen (and be possible) when the leadership is leaning in.

Leaders have to open the door to the conversation. As a leader, you have to show that you "get it" or at the very least that you want to "get it."

My favourite client story is about a leader who "gets it." We met at a community event. It was a town hall type meeting for members of the LGBTQ2SI+ communities who are also racialized, and it was specifically to discuss the disparity of black children in the child welfare system in Ontario (the One Vision, One Voice[36] initiative).

---

[35] https://fivetonine.co/blog/erg-inclusion-strategy (accessed April 29, 2020)

[36] http://www.oacas.org/what-we-do/onevisiononevoice/ (accessed August 9, 2020)

We were asked to sit at round tables and were given questions to discuss. The person sitting next to me was an executive director of a children's aid agency. The first thing she said after she introduced herself to the people at the table was that she was there to listen. I rolled my eyes internally. *Sure you are,* I thought to myself. *We'll see.* But to her credit, she did just that. She understood that this wasn't her space to talk and that she had much to learn. And her words created the opportunity for her to hear some stories she may otherwise not have heard as a white woman. Those stories helped her to see more, understand more, and furthered her commitment to change. As a result of that leaning in, we ended up working together and creating change in her agency.

So, it's not a problem if work colleagues gravitate towards each other because of similarity. The challenge is if this separation is *systemic.*

Questions to Ponder

1. How do your organizational systems group people together?

2. Do you have Employee Resource Groups (ERGs)? If so, how are they contributing to their people and to the organization? If not, why not?

3. How can your leadership partner with your black ERGs to help increase awareness and understanding—and support a stronger organizational commitment to understanding and challenging systemic anti-black racism and systemic racism?

CHAPTER 7

New Mission: Be More Black

The year my daughter turned four and started school was the same year I started exploring what it meant to be black and my lack of blackness. This didn't happen because of her, but it happened in tandem with her school experiences and her growing awareness that she looked different than many of her classmates, and that this wasn't always considered by others to be a good thing.

In the spring of that year, I met a man at a conference. He is black and Native American. We had a brief, whirlwind long-distance affair that lasted only four months, and he ended it abruptly over the phone. It was a call that blew my life open. Because the reason I was dumped—in part—was because I wasn't black enough.

Not Black Enough (What We Miss When We Don't See the Whole Person)

Don't tell me I'm not black enough

What does that mean, anyway?
Are you judging my oppression
based on shade?

What about my brownness?
The word I lovingly used
because black isn't who I am,
not allowed to be,
not here

It's true that my lighter skin
gives me privilege;
I have access where you may not,
I may pass where you cannot,
and I move through the world
differently
because of those

But my skin is not white

I'm still a person of colour
which means, in the world today,
I'm still "less than"

But you don't see me

you don't see my brownness;
you see my whiteness

When you tell me
I'm not black enough,
what you are saying
is that I can't know your pain,
your heart,
your songs,
your struggle

But...

Somewhere inside
the fibers of my being,
the resistance is awake
itching

Looking for a way to speak
that doesn't speak over you

Looking for a way to weep
that doesn't deny you the space

Hoping for a place to belong

Your words erase
the part of me
that is black,
the part that I have struggled
all of my life
to be

You don't see me

I remember where I was standing when I took the break-up call, the brightness of the September sky, the sharp colours of the flowers in the garden, and how everything disappeared around me as I heard the words that would change my life and set me on a new path.

"You are too comfortable in white spaces," he said.

Too White (The Way We Keep Others Separate)

My "white side"
has kept me
from being with you,
laughing with you,
learning with you
— and also healing with you

It has kept me
away,
kept me
at a distance,
made me feel
small,
allowed me,
in moments,
to feel big

Worst of all,
it has meant
that I have had
no place
to weep
for my brothers and sisters,
except alone

I have had
no place
to rail against
injustice,
except alone

I have pressed
my nose
against the glass
of your blackness
and have watched you,
and you have not let me in

And now you judge me for that

"You are too comfortable in white spaces" felt like an accusation.

I defended myself by pointing out that unlike where he lived, in a US city with a large black population, I didn't have that same luxury here in Toronto to choose *not* to be around people who are white.

But the truth, I know now, is bigger than this; how, where, and by whom I was raised has had an impact. I am comfortable in white spaces because those are the spaces I have mostly been in (and continue to be, although to a lesser degree). I know the rules. My light skin privilege grants me entry and some acceptance. Much of these early spaces—neighbourhoods, schools—were ones I didn't choose. For some, like my choice of university, I wasn't conscious enough about "race" to make a different decision. And others didn't feel like a choice because of the specter of not feeling black enough.

As a mother, I have tried to make sure my child feels comfortable in both white and black spaces. Much of this is because of our family, my circle of friends and chosen family, but also in my choice of events and activities. My hope is that she will feel comfortable in her skin and comfortable in any space—and not feel the loneliness, disconnect and feeling of not belonging anywhere that I have felt as a "biracial" person.

I have spent my life wanting to be more black. Those seven words—"You are too comfortable in white spaces"—showed me not only that I still wasn't black enough but also *how white I am.*

The words, and his rejection, cracked me open and blew a hole through me so wide that for about eight weeks, I lost my footing.

And then, I started to wonder how—*if* - I could raise my brown child well.

I Am My Mother in This Story (How We Replicate What We Know, Without Realizing It)

I didn't consider
that the same
lack of experience
that kept me apart
may also keep
my child apart

I'm the one
not providing
a black experience
now

I don't cook the right food,
listen to the right music,
embody the right sense of colour

I can't teach her a gaze
that isn't fully mine

Do I know how to raise a strong black girl?

Oh my God…
I'm my mother in this story!

Perhaps I should have had a white child after all…

Acceptance in White Spaces

The truth is that white spaces feel easier for me. I know the rules. I am just different enough to be noticed but not *so* different that I'm pushed too far away. There is a cost for that, of course; I'm never fully relaxed because I am aware of my skin colour, and if I choose to speak up from my non-white lens, I'm conscious of what I say. But it's a dance that I know. It's easy for me to determine what not to say and what not to share. I keep many thoughts to myself in general, so this is second nature.

In black spaces, however, I have the opposite problem of not knowing what to say. And worrying that what I *do* say will be insufficient. I feel inadequate and ever conscious of saying the wrong thing, of outing myself as less than. I always feel like I'm pressing my face up against the glass, wishing I was closer, wanting to be closer, and feeling apart-from. Consequently, I am always grateful, relieved, and a little surprised when I'm welcomed in and asked to stay. I realize in those moments that I've been holding my breath.

I don't have that same feeling of hesitancy in white spaces—except around my sexual orientation and deciding if I want to come out as queer. In white spaces, I'm always aware of my skin colour and the way it removes me—even slightly—from the circle. But it doesn't keep me from those spaces (unless there is a reason for fear). I want to say, "How could it?" given where I live. But there is more to this. I have simply taken for granted—despite the difference I feel—that I will fit in.

When my daughter was three years old, I was introduced to the German School in Toronto. We were invited to the Christmas Bazaar. I briefly considered sending her there to solidify the base in German she had received from my mom when she was a baby. But I didn't want her to be the only non-white kid in the school. My father told me not to limit her experiences.

I was worried about her self-esteem. He was worried about much more.

But I digress.

At many points in my life, I didn't have a choice of what spaces I was in. My father's family is spread out across Jamaica, the US, and Canada. I grew up in predominantly white neighbourhoods and went to schools with little diversity in culture or skin tone. Because we moved to Ontario from Quebec when I was 12, my parents' social network disappeared and entertaining or visiting family friends (of all skin colours and cultures) evaporated.

As an adult, the narrative of "not black enough" has been very strong. I didn't feel I had the right to ask for entry into black spaces. I was too different, too "not black." And the older I got, the more foreign black spaces felt. The gap that was evident in Nicole's basement in Grade 3 had grown significantly.

So, this man's accusation of comfort was accurate. But what he missed was my pain. And it was that pain that started to seep from me.

I wept, sat with shame, and felt the years of my childhood and the separateness from my Caribbean family run through me.

What Do You See?—Part 1 (The Impact of Colour Blindness, Racism, and Stereotypes)

White brother,
what do you see?

Those that love me
see nothing
don't see my colour
and don't understand
that this is not
a good thing

Those that
don't love me
see black
maybe brown
maybe they don't know
what I am,
but they know
I'm not
one of them

Here are the things
I am meant to know
in white spaces
– spice and dance

My skin is envied
and because I have
"good hair"
it is envied too

Being Brown in a Black and White World

*But no one sees me
because my colour
has no voice here*

*And anyway,
I can't stay*

*I can't breathe deeply here
although I want to*

*It seems like
such a happy place*

What Do You See?—Part 2

Black brother,
what do you see?

In black spaces
I don't know enough,
the right things to say,
the lyrics,
And my hips don't lie

I have no context
on which
to rest my unease,
my anger,
my sadness

And all that
you see
is the melanin
that is missing
not me
not the passion,
the power,
the fire

Because I'm hiding
here too
hoping my voice,
my tongue,
my lack of cultural reference,
the sound of my mother's culture
doesn't strip me

of the opportunity
to be with you

Sometimes it does,
and I am set adrift
again

Sometimes it doesn't,
and I have a moment
of rest

Until the next time

Eventually, through an email exchange, I came to understand that beyond my experience of not being black enough, there was a gaze I was missing. Although I have mentioned it in previous chapters, this is the moment where that awareness began.

This realization made me incredibly sad, and it made sense. I don't see the world as a person who is black because I have never felt like someone who is black, and haven't been seen as someone who is black by the people in my life who are. My upbringing and circumstances mean I have been trained to use a white gaze. My skin tone means I do have a person of colour gaze. But it's not a black gaze.

This left me feeling even more inadequate. But it gave me an entry point. I bought many books about racism and segregation. The mere presence of these books on my bookshelf felt like a silent nod to half of my ancestors.

And then I met Bea and dropped into a deeper place in my journey.

I was invited by a colleague, Candy Barone, to attend her leadership workshop in Texas. I would provide the "D&I lens." I was thrilled and pleased to see a few familiar faces in the room.

As we all went around and introduced ourselves, Bea, the only African American present, shared her feelings as she walked from her car that morning (*Would she be the only African American there? Did she have the energy?*) and the hope that rose when she saw one of the workshop participants who had kinky hair, but white skin; *maybe, she wouldn't be alone.* During this sharing, another colleague shot me a look that suggested she was confused, that Bea had missed me in her assessment of racial representation. It was a silent question, but I answered out loud.

"Don't look at me," I said. "I'm not African American!"

The room stopped. And I wished the floor would swallow me up.

While it is true— I'm not African American —the outburst was fueled by my pain. She hadn't seen me. Once again, I wasn't black enough to even make it onto the racial radar. The result was that I made it a point to avoid Bea for the whole two-day workshop. I didn't make eye contact, I made sure to choose other people as partners when required to do so, and there was no chitchat during breaks or lunch. I skillfully maneuvered myself around the room to ensure we didn't connect.

And then, I didn't have a choice.

She Hugged Me, and I Cried (Why Representation is Important)

I didn't want to hug her
but I had to
it was part of
the workshop closing

So, I saved her for last
hardly looked at her
as I walked closer

But when I got close
and my arms
landed around her shoulders
I sunk in
held on
felt all the hugs
I never had
from my grandmother
from my aunties

I felt what it was like
to be held
tightly
to be safe
to be home

I cried

For all the hugs
I have missed,
will never have,
but for which
my soul longs

This meeting (and our ensuing conversations and connection) was healing for me because my awareness moved from an intellectual exercise to my heart. All of the books on my shelf at home had provided some insight, but in that hug, I sunk into the pain of segmentation and separation, the pain that not being black enough has meant to my *soul*.

Here is the thing about soul pain. It snakes around you like a shadow, whispering. It doesn't leave you alone until you stop what you are doing, notice and pay attention. Meeting Bea stopped me in my tracks; I *had* to pay attention. And what I was beginning to see was bigger than my desire to be "more black"; what I saw was that a part of me was missing.

The impact of this on me as a mother was profound; *what was my child missing as a result?*

I felt inadequate; I felt sad, and I was afraid. *What if I couldn't provide her with what she needed to become a strong woman of colour? What if my lack of blackness translated into another generation of misplaced melanin and searching for a place to belong?*

Thankfully I'm not the only parent, but I am *Mom…*

Are You Raising Your Daughter Black?

"Are you raising
your daughter black?"
You (a strong
successful
black woman)
ask me
on our way out the door

I don't know
how to tell you
that I don't know
what that means

I want to say
"How can I?"
But your question
has me feeling
small

So I say
"I'm trying"
which I think
we both know
means "No"

I'm not equipped
to raise my daughter black
to raise a black daughter

when I'm not

This new and at times overwhelming journey called parenting collided with identity, and it occurred to me that there was much I didn't know (and much I felt I *needed* to know) in order to raise my daughter with a stronger sense of awareness of who she is.

The challenge was that if I dug into my own childhood experiences, I came up short.

I Was Raised by White People

I was raised by white people.

The childhood memories
that make me smile
– really smile from my belly
– are of Austria

The mountains

The stream
where I dropped my
10 Little Rabbits *book*
and we ran to catch it
on the other side of the bridge

The pool
where they sold ice cream
and I was perhaps the first
person of colour
in that tiny town

Playing ping-pong
with my cousins
in name only,
not by blood,
But it didn't matter

My first crush

I love the accordion
I speak dialect,
not "proper German"

It's all part of me
A part I feel
distant from now
because of the melanin
in my skin

As if denying
that part
makes me more
of what I'm not,
more of what
I've longed to be

I wonder what
I would feel like
if I had as many
childhood memories
of Jamaica
and that side
of my family;
if I wasn't trying
so hard
to catch up
and make up
for lack of experience

As if soaking it up now
could make me more
of what I'm not

I was raised
by white people

What colour
does that make me?

It occurred to me then that the intense focus I had on having a child who looked like me, so we would be received by others as a unit (unlike my childhood experiences), meant that I had missed a crucial element. *What could I teach her about being black? What gaze would she have? And how was I going to make sure she didn't come up short like I felt I had?*

I remember the intensity of my tears one early morning. Everyone else was still asleep, and our home was quiet as I sat on the couch, terrified I was not going to be able to raise my child well enough to become a strong black woman. I was touching the edges of the racial dance I had been doing my whole life. No entry for me into black spaces meant that maybe I was compromising her entry too.

Creating Safe Spaces at Work

While I spent much of my life trying to "be more black," the reality for people who are black is that because we live in a society built on systemic racism, to "make it" often requires being *less* black. Because the black narrative we are fed in subtle and not so subtle ways suggests that being black is less than, "making it" is synonymous with whiteness and the things that go with it.

When I think about the workplace in that light, I wonder how effective it can be to create an inclusive environment when the undertones of whiteness run so deep. Are we welcoming people who aren't white to be all of who they are at work, or are we still—even with a commitment to D&I—going to expect them to be less like themselves to "make it"?

What are the subtle cues that are embedded in your culture that suggests to an employee of colour or an employee who is black that they need to change who they are to succeed?

That is not what the essence of inclusion means. Creating an inclusive environment means that we don't have to change who we are to be granted entry or to shine. But how many times have you heard "fit" used in your workplace as a reason for not hiring or not promoting someone—or for letting them go? "Fit" is this slippery, vague word that we get away with using instead of saying what it is about the person that we don't like, that we find unsettling, that suggests they are not "like us".

The whole point of diversity and inclusion is that we learn, grow, and go further when difference is embraced. Research tells us that it is inclusion that increases:

- Engagement

- Productivity

- Satisfaction

And yet, I find that companies focus on the diversity, hoping it will lead to these benefits, and miss the point that with diversity comes differences beyond appearance. And that these perspectives, experiences, and insights are precisely what create:

- Opportunity

- Innovation

- Change

If we are hiring people who look different and then requiring them to "act like us" or to "fit," we are missing the point.

Often when companies lean into D&I, what they are asking of employees of colour and employees who are black is to be less of who they are in order to make it easier for everyone else (read: the white employees) to continue to be who *they* are, and for things to continue as they have.

If I have learned anything in these past few years, it's that being anything other than who we are limits our effectiveness and stifles our genius.

Systemic racism and systemic anti-black racism do this on a grand scale.

Questions to Ponder

1. What does "fit" look like in your organization or company?

2. What does your work culture say to your employees about who and what is "acceptable" (or not)?

3. What are the subtle and unofficial ways that you build connection, mentor, and create community with people in your organization or company? With whom does this happen, and who is left out (and why)?

4. What could you be missing as a result of all of the above?

Consider what you could do to widen your ability to see the richness people bring—because of who they are—that you may be squashing by requiring "fit."

CHAPTER 8

"Mom, I Want to be White"

Isn't it interesting that during the time I was diving into my blackness, my daughter was about to start school and would quickly turn her back on hers?

At a birthday party during the summer my daughter turned four, a child who is white commented on her "crazy hair." Suddenly, my child started refusing to wear her hair out, feeling self-conscious about her incredible, thick curls.

In senior-kindergarten, she started wanting straight hair.

And by Grade 1, she was talking about wanting to be white.

I was beside myself.

What am I doing wrong?

She was surrounded by people who are black and people of colour in our family and friend circles. We had books at home with black characters.

Given my experience, the only thing I was well-equipped for was to address her hair trauma.

I understand, on a visceral level, what it's like to want straight hair. Look around—the female standard of beauty in North American society (and in many cases, globally) is (still) to be white, thin, blonde, and with straight hair. These are the images we see the most when we walk by any magazine rack. The majority of characters on TV, in movies, and in cartoons meet that criteria. That's white supremacy in action.

I have what is called "good hair" in the black community; it's curly, but not as kinky as "black hair." It's a label that is a legacy of colonization and white supremacy—where white characteristics are the standard to aspire to. My paternal grandmother was apparently pleased about this when I was born, and she also had "good hair."

But "good hair" is only good when you are familiar with the hair it is supposedly better than. My mother was not. And my father didn't do hair. As a result, none of us knew my hair's potential. I have far too many school pictures to prove that: fuzz, frizz, inappropriate hairstyles, lack of hairstyles and many, many years of ponytails (that didn't "swish" when I moved).

Despite my "good hair" as a teenager, I spent my money on hair relaxer that burned my nose and my scalp so I could have that "hair blowing in the breeze" feeling, use a curling iron (yes, for real!), and be able to run my fingers through it like the girls on the TV shows I watched and books I read suggested I should be able to do, to be beautiful.

In university, I had my undergrad graduation picture taken with my hair wet, so it was curly and not frizzy or fuzzy. And then a few years later, I cut my hair short, so my curls weren't an issue. I felt liberated. I sported that short style, on and off, for about 15 years.

When I was 46, I found the Curl Ambassadors[37] and finally learned about the ways and products that respect the curl. Understanding how to take care of my curly hair was a life-changing experience. I finally felt beautiful. I finally had hair (and a hairstyle) that I loved. And I was thankful to be able to pass the knowledge on to my child. Part of me thought it was too early for her to be using hair products, but when she smiled at herself (and me) in the mirror and said, "I love my hair," my heart sang.

So, I understand my daughter's hair pain. I know what it feels like to wish the wind wasn't your enemy, that you didn't require a spray bottle to fix the style you took too many minutes mastering before you stepped out the door, and that just for once, you could make your hair look like the style in the magazine. I know why she wants her hair free in the pool so she can feel it move in the water.

What I *didn't* understand was my child's desire to be white.

I spoke about it with some friends who are black. *What was I doing wrong?* I wanted to know. The answers I got shouldn't have surprised me: "In a world where whiteness is 'the standard,'" they told me, "It makes sense that she wants to be white."

Ah…

What Does Whiteness Mean?

Black and white are not just colours. They are not just skin colours. They come with a whole narrative and

---

37   https://curlambassadors.ca/

ways of being. Whiteness is the standard according to which all are measured. White supremacy, at its core, is a concept - not an action or a title or a group.

We see this concept played out daily. Walk past a magazine rack; it will tell you all you need to know about white supremacy. Most of the covers are people who are white. Many of the women have blonde hair. And my daughter knew it at age four.

Whiteness as the standard means that looks and ways of being (including talking, extracurricular activities, food and music, as well as things like education, parenting, how we work, and work culture) are measured against what these are for people who are white.

The result is a perpetual sense of falling short for people who are black and people of colour—because the rules and things used to measure success have not been made with their ways of being in mind.

Questions to Ponder

1. How does whiteness creep into your organizational culture?

2. By what standard are you measuring value, input, and success?

3. What can you do to dig into the essence of what you are looking for (for a position) without attaching a skin colour to it?

CHAPTER 9

Cracking Open (What if I Can Just Be Me?)

This is the turning point—the moment where everything changed in an instant. In June of 2019 I was in Winnipeg at a business retreat run by my friend and colleague Joseph Ranseth, who teaches people how to start movements.

But before I tell you the story, let me preface it by letting you know that at the time of the retreat I had been planning a trip to Austria that summer for my mother, my daughter, and me. As a result, many memories and thoughts were swirling around in my mind about "race," belonging, racism, family, and wondering what my child who wanted to be white would feel like in a country surrounded by people who (almost exclusively) are. I was a little worried about her sense of self, and curious about mine.

As I sat in a café in Montreal the month before— another place filled with ghosts of my former self—I contemplated the many emotions I was feeling about our upcoming trip.

Pre-Austria Musings—Part 1

In less than eight weeks,
we are going to Austria

Austria!

Flashes sneak up on me:
my aunt's schnitzel
the taste of her salad
the smell of her kitchen
the forest
the mountains
cows

I'm a brown girl
with an Austrian heart
I don't get these feelings
about Jamaica
I don't have childhood memories
that are rooted there

This makes me sad
confused
ashamed
but I can't capture
what I never had
and that makes me sadder

What if…

No amount of jerk chicken,
reggae

or sorrel–making
will give me entry
to a place
I didn't learn as a child
and that is not in my bones

But Austria…

I feel like
I'm not supposed
to love this country
of mountains,
beer,
white people,
and reminders
of genocide

I'm sure my white grandfather
would be horrified
to see where his genetics
ended up

But here I am
sitting in a café
a world away,
sending emails
to cousins
with eager anticipation
of seeing them again

And feeling torn
about what my heart

and my skin
don't have in common

Looking like I do,
and with the history
of colonization,
I shouldn't feel
like I belong there

That's what I tell myself

And then I wonder
if that's my self-imposed box
or the box society has offered
that I have voluntarily
stepped into

Pre-Austria Musings—Part 2

I'm going back
to Austria,
the land I spent
a few long, lazy
family-filled
summers in
as a child
and teenager

The place where I
tasted freedom,
learned that cows
have personalities
and different faces,
where I saw how bread
was made,
and how the tile
in the old farmhouse
kitchen floor
came out
so my aunt could
step down
and see inside
that old wood fire oven

It's where I learned
that my mom
can recognize
mushrooms
in the woods
that are edible,

and where I saw
remnants of Roman roads
across the mountains

Evidence of history

Not mine

It's also where
I endured
finger-pointing
out of curiosity
which caused me
to feel
conspicuous
different
not "one of"

Other

I don't look
like I belong there,
but I sound like I could,
and I feel like I do

It's a complicated history
I have with a country
I have no business
belonging to

This was where I was at, and on the heels of this planning and anticipation, I found myself in Winnipeg for a few days at the end of June. On my second morning there, and the first morning of the retreat, I decided to skip the group breakfast in favour of a walk by the river. Something was calling, although I wasn't sure what it was.

I had paper and a pencil with me like I used to on morning walks with my dog years ago. I knew from experience that moments of inspiration land quietly but quickly, and it's good to be prepared.

As I walked, I left the paved path and walked onto the riverbank. I found a low branch to sit on and looked out over the water. Eventually, I felt a poem coming on, so I took out my paper and pencil and began to write.

Holla at Me—Part 1

"Holla at me," you said

It took me a moment

I wish I could
I don't even know
if I'm spelling it right

How about I call you?
or text?

I wish I was black
wish my body moved
in acknowledgment
of my ancestors
Wish more of the food
was familiar
or a staple

Wish my skin
was darker
or my hair
more kinky

So I could holla at you
so I could feel like I could
so I would do it right

When I wish for these things
the white part of me
is forgotten

takes a back seat,
and I am only
realizing now
that this might mean
it has the front seat
when I'm not wishing

Holla at Me—Part 2

Holla-ing at you
is just the beginning

When we connect
you will find
that I don't know
the right words,
have the right
inflection,
or understand the phrases
you may use
…or their history

And then I will feel
the whiteness
under my skin,
and you'll see it

Because maybe
until then
you had hope,
thought we had more
in common,
because of my colour

And I'll feel sorry
to disappoint
and like the outsider
I am
all over again

So, a correction:

I don't long to be different
just more of who I am
more of the half
that darkens my skin
more than melanin

I am missing the soul of half my people

And I want it back

"Holla at me" was something my daughter's teacher, who is black, said to me at school a few days before. We were talking about shoes and my favourite store. "Holla at me" was her invitation to me to let her know when the next sale was on. And here it was, having made its way through my being, onto the page.

I didn't expect this poem. The sadness that I had begun to feel years earlier while talking with Bea was back in these lines, and it still gripped me.

At the retreat later that day, as we spoke about our work and our businesses, I happened to mention the poem and was asked to read it. Because I was among friends, I obliged. I felt awkward in a room of three white men to be reading about such personal racial pain. *What do they know?* I wondered silently. But as I read, I saw the words land; I saw the emotion in their eyes and felt it in the energy of the room. This surprised me, although I know it shouldn't have. Pain, after all, is universal.

After a moment, Joseph asked me a few questions, during which I shared the story (and my frustration) of my daughter wanting to be white. I recounted the day when we walked across the street on the way home from school, over the zebra stripes, past the crossing guard. She was skipping happily and holding my hand when she nonchalantly announced, "I love white people."

My breath stopped. *What am I doing wrong,* I wondered, *that my brown-skinned child not only wants to be white but loves white people?* In that moment, I felt her words viscerally, and they hurt. *What was I teaching my child involuntarily?* I wanted to know, *that she wasn't telling me she loved black people?*

As I recounted the story that afternoon in Winnipeg, surrounded by neon sticky notes about business offerings and different coloured markers, I could feel the same incredulity and shame. Given what I do in the world, given how conscious I had been to have a brown child, given who I have surrounded her with, I felt like I had failed. I laughed bitterly, but what I wanted to do was cry.

One of Joseph's questions gave me pause.

He simply asked, "What if everything is perfect?"

What if Everything Is Perfect?

What if everything is perfect?
I am asked
from across the table

I have just shared
my heartbreak
my railing against injustice
my shame
as a mother
and a D&I consultant

My brown daughter has told me
she loves white people
on the heels of wanting
to be white

"What if everything is perfect?"

Perfect?
How?

I wait
for what, I don't know

It's a slow dawning

The tears surprise me
as the words come

"I would say,
'That's wonderful honey,'"

I want her to love people
all people

"So, what is she teaching you?"

The room waits
I wait

I have wanted
to be black
all my life

I now see
that this means
that I have also
not wanted
to be white

How did I miss that?

Running to
also means
running from

Not enough,
not good enough,
not what I want

"I have to love
the white in me,"
I said
"Wrap my arms around myself,
both parts,
and love it all,"

Oh...

It felt like everything changed that afternoon. Something opened. Some part of me that had been locked away felt like it took its first breath. The world felt different.

I felt different.

I wasn't sure I liked it, and I didn't know what to do with myself.

Who Am I? (If We Aren't "Racial", What Are We?)

I miss the struggle

Without it
I have to define
who I am
by both
not by what
I am not

I can't pit one
against the other
to gain acceptance

I can't forget one
in favour of silence

My voice
will be different now

Both

Over time
as I hold them
–hold me–
I will know more
of what that means

But for now,
I feel a peace
I have longed for

Black
and white
room for both

Breathe

Nothing to prove
no shame
acceptance

My ancestors are smiling
as they all gather
around the fire
making room

Now the party begins

Of course, that was easier said than done. I had 49 years to unlearn. I am still doing so. This was not an intellectual exercise either; it was something I felt, some shift that happened that I followed, with hope and trepidation.

Do You See Me? (What We Miss When We Don't Consider Skin Colour)

"Do you see me?"
white asked

How can I not?

You are everywhere:
in what I know
how I speak
what I wear
how I move
in my gaze
what I notice
and what I miss

I can't help but see you

Even when I have
seen black
I have seen you
in the absence of
what I am there

"Do you love me?"

I have not

I have blamed you
for all the things
I am not
am missing

long to know
have
be

But I will love you now,
white
because now I see
that doing so
makes the black I am
show up,
and then
I can love you both

To My White Side

Instead of being grateful
for what you have given me:
privilege
"good hair"
a second language
a sense of home
I didn't want those,
and I have hated you
for the things I perceived
you had taken from me

Because of you
I wasn't black enough
I didn't fit
was apart from
instead of a part of
I missed the embrace
of my grandmother
and a feeling of home
in the place of my
father's birth

Or so I thought

Because I was focused
on what I lacked
I could not embrace
what I had

I have wasted my time
mourning something
I can never be,
was not meant to be,
instead of celebrating
who I am
and what that means

Black is more
than a colour

And it's not my skin
that has
betrayed me

I blamed you, white
and kept apart
from black

Instead of holding
and nurturing
what black I had
I let it go
as not enough

So that in the end
I didn't love
either of you

And haven't loved me

What if We Stopped Seeing "Other" and Made Room for "Both"?

This section started with pain, but it transformed. And the transformation was the realization that by wanting to be more black, I was also wanting to be less white. And ultimately, I am both. It is in holding that both, in resisting the familiar urge to be either/or, one or the other, that I have begun to find peace.

I see the same struggle in the world. Black *or* white. Us *or* them. We are always being asked to choose. As if there isn't room for all of us—people of mixed "race" especially.

We may tell ourselves, as people who are black, as people of colour, that we have to stay apart from white people because of the pain of colonization and slavery. We may tell ourselves not to trust, to look at the broken system, and take caution. We have learned from experience. And the experience is *real*. The broken system – the system of caste as Isabel Wilkerson writes about in her book by that name - is *real*. Ask any of your employees who are black or of colour about their journey, and they will tell you stories of how real it is.

But "race" is not real. It's a convenient fabrication to make lighter skin more valued, and then made the transatlantic slave trade palatable to those who profited from it. And it stuck, so the value-system could continue—right up to today—without people seeing how it has broken the human soul.

We are all human beings. "Races" are fabricated. But we have been fragmented based on melanin, told ourselves (and have been subjected to) made-up stories to keep us disconnected, and we *all* lose.

Remember that Einstein told us that we couldn't fix the problem with the same consciousness in which it was created.

I am learning to live in the middle, in the both/and. I'm breathing into it because the either/or will continue to tear me apart—will continue to tear *us* apart. It tears us apart as a society, as people in organizations, and as families.

In companies where systemic racism/anti-black racism manifests itself so obviously in who is in leadership and who is not, who is on the front line, and who is not, how processes and experiences are different based on skin colour, it's easy to see the impact of either/or thinking.

The organizational transformation comes when we begin to not only see each other but also see the divide and make space for both/and. This means that we have to be willing to hear stories, listen, acknowledge pain, ask questions, and learn.

We have to be willing to walk through the mess together.

Both/and means we *all* win.

Questions to Ponder

1. Do you include demographics in your employee engagement surveys, and do you disaggregate the data by skin colour to see the difference in experience?

2. If you do, what do you do with the data? How do you show people that you hear and see them, and how have you begun the process of change?

3. If you don't see the divide, who can help you see it so that you can work towards bridging the gap?

CHAPTER 10

A White Man Taught Me that "Race" Isn't Real

It's true.

I have known for a long time that "race" is a social construct. But it took until age 49 for it to really sink into me, in a way that resonated.

On the heels of my ah-hah moment in Winnipeg, my mother, daughter, and I hopped on a plane and flew across the Atlantic Ocean to Austria to visit our relatives—my mother's family. I had some trepidation about this trip. For my part, I had so many beautiful memories, and along with these a curiosity about how I would fit, having moved further into blackness and then with my recent opening about holding both. I also wondered how my child would feel, surrounded by no one who looked like her except me.

But I was also flying over with a greater awareness of wholeness—a different awareness—thanks to Randy Harris. He runs a website called Understanding Compassion, where he has a ten-part article series on "race."[38] Because of his experience (as a white man) with

---

[38]   https://understandingcompassion.com/education/

this curriculum (for which he received permission to turn into these articles), he is on a mission to have a course on "race" in every high school in the USA. He believes knowledge will help end racism.

Due to conversations over months with him and two of our colleagues about his mission, and through these articles, I shed another layer of the myth that we have all grown up in: that skin colours separate us into different "races." This was not a new phenomenon for me. I have known that "race" is a social construct since grad school. A few years before, I attended a "Beyond Race" workshop in New York City where we learned about the classification of human beings into "races" using skulls and geography, and how a switch to colour versus location in these "race" names made it easier to then discriminate against (and dehumanize) people who were black.[39] I knew all of this, intellectually. I think what happened on my trip (post-Winnipeg retreat) was a collision of many things, that allowed this knowing to finally land firmly in my heart.

The result was a new sense, not that I was made of two halves, not that I wasn't enough of one or too much of the other, but a quiet settling in to the knowing that I am simply who I am—a human being with a particular skin tone born of genetics gifted to me by my parents. Not as half black and half white, not as less of one and more of the other, not part of anything—*I am all me.* The beauty of this learning—and the fact that it

---

[39] You can read more about this in Rodney Patterson's book *Trumping the Race Card: A National Agenda - Moving Beyond Race and Racism*

happened when it did— allowed me to see myself in a completely different way, "Whole, instead of being half of something," as the Proclaimers sang.[40]

I felt free.

---

[40] Song lyrics from "Then I Met You" by the Proclaimers: Sunshine on Leith album (2011)

Black and White

As if white and black
are separate colours
mixed together
to make me
us
browns, "biracials," mixed "race"

When there are no "races"
just human beings
with different
amounts of melanin,
it changes the story

Who do I get to be now?

In a world
that hasn't learned this yet
and still wants
to define me by my skin
–a shallow definition–
when melanin runs high

It's only defining contribution?
A shade

Not a culture
a history
a people
like white

Pre-Austria Musings—Part 3

My skin colour
would tell you
I'm not supposed to understand
what 'pfirti' means
or know how to make strudl
But I do

And my heart leaps
when I hear
the accordion playing…
the accordion!

It's either a cruel joke
or a flash of insight
by something greater
than me

Or maybe
my analysis
is an
oversimplification
based on a
social construct

When it is, in fact
a much more
complicated process

A process that includes
family
place

time
and memory

Despite colour

Maybe that's
the lesson
I'm here to learn
and share

That colour
doesn't matter,
and does matter
at the same time...

Labels, "Race," and the Workplace

The fact that "race" is a social construct landed in my bones on my trip to Austria. This was powerful learning for me. It's fascinating how knowledge gets buried—hidden—until the time comes when we can truly access it.

The articles on Randy Harris' website contain information that I have already known, some of it for longer, some for less time. But there was something magical about reading it when I did, after the crack and while in Austria.

The beauty of the message, for me, was watching the peeling away of the label from who I am. If "races" don't exist, I can't be not enough of something or too much of something else. It allows me to just be me. It gives me freedom.

Human beings like to label things. Perhaps, it gives us comfort. Perhaps, it allows us to categorize or know how to treat someone. The problem is that labels ultimately put us into boxes. Those may not be consistent over time or people, but they are constricting, nevertheless.

In a workplace, like any other place, we take this label of "race," and because of the reality of racism (and what we have been taught, overtly and covertly as a result), we make skin colour mean things. In a workplace, some of these meanings include who will be a good worker, who we can trust, who will be responsible, who will make a good manager, who will give us trouble, who we can promote, to whom we can speak about certain things, who won't "get it," who will "fit," and who will not.

These meanings inform how we treat people, how we interact with each other, what we expect, and what we will give. Simply put, the myth about "race" and the caste system created with this myth has allowed people who are black and people of colour to be mistreated, set aside, excluded, discounted, ignored, even killed—all while *justified* because someone decided melanin made a person "less than", for convenience and profit.

We do this in schools and in families and in communities as well. Consciously and unconsciously—because unconscious bias is one of the manifestations of systemic racism.

These labels are passed on—from generation to generation, within families, communities, societies and the world—meaning we don't interrogate them, see them critically for what they are, and we can't get out from under them. And because our brain is all about efficiency, those meanings become mental associations and then become what we use to make split decisions—to some people's benefit and to other people's detriment.

Unconscious bias is a very popular subject in workplace diversity and inclusion circles, with good reason, because it greatly undermines inclusion efforts if left unchecked and unexplored. One of the biggest unconscious beliefs that we hold, collectively, is that there are different "races" in the world. And with that, a hierarchy of value—with light skin being on the top and dark skin being on the bottom, and a gradient of shades in between. It's the most insidious of myths that has caused (and continues to perpetuate) anti-black racism and racism and, with it, unnecessary suffering, disconnection, and pain for everyone, some on the receiving end as dark-skinned and others by virtue of what they will miss as light-skinned.

Companies and organizations miss out on innovation, creativity, diversity of thought, varied perspectives and ideas, and opportunities. Because we see people through a narrow lens of skin colour that we have been taught is about "race" and is ultimately tied to value. When we set aside the myth, we have the opportunity to not only see people for who they are and what they have to offer but we also create the opportunity for greater connection.

Questions to Ponder

1. Can you imagine having a conversation about "race"? If not, why not?

2. What would you need to support a conversation about "race"?

3. What do you have in place organizationally to mitigate unconscious bias?

CHAPTER 11

Coming Home...In Austria?!

The irony is clear; after 49 years of wanting to be more black, I learned a huge lesson about belonging in one of the whitest countries in the world.

I wondered about this trip. I was curious, nervous, excited, and cautious. Something felt different this time; *I* felt different. And my child was three years older than the last time we were in Austria, and seemingly not comfortable in her skin.

We would be gone for three weeks—a tour of all the relatives, many living in tiny towns with no traffic lights, and no racial diversity at all. Part of me remembered what it felt like to be the main attraction, and I had to breathe deeply. Part of me was looking forward to seeing my family and breathing the mountain air.

But I did wonder what the trip would be like, how *I* would be on the trip: Going to this place I love, with this new awareness. I hoped for openness, so I could learn what I needed to.

Because I don't believe in coincidences...

Anticipation

I am going to Austria
the land I love
my heart is happy
and the many childhood
memories
flood me
and bring me
advanced joy

Mountains
cows
chocolate
hazelnut ice cream
hiking
schnitzl

How will I be this time
without apology
for being brown
and with awareness
of how I fit?

Will it be
a different experience?
Or will I
just be different?

Let me hear
and see things
through the lens of
both/and

let me experience things
as black <u>and</u> white

And see how it feels
to live in <u>all</u> of my skin

One of my first lessons and ah-hah moments on this trip happened on the plane. I decided to watch the movie *The Hate U Give* that was available as an airline media movie selection.

Greatness, Explained

"Don't you forget that being black is an honour because we come from greatness."

*– From the movie The Hate U Give
(based on the book by Angie Thomas)*

*I hear the words
take them in
nod*

*What a change
from two weeks ago
when
the lump in my throat
touched on
'not enough'
'why not me'
And 'if only'*

*This time
the words
feel like
they are also
for me*

Even if just partly

This was a new experience for me—an *in*. I cried as I watched *The Hate U Give* on the plane, and saw the "talk" that the father has with his two young children as the movie begins. I wondered what it would have been like to have a talk like that, acknowledging all of who I am. But I took it in, even just a little, and let the words sprinkle love and acceptance over me.

Once we landed, I continued my personal journey with "race," reading the articles on the *Understanding Compassion* website on the train as the Austrian countryside rattled past and in the wee hours in my uncle and aunt's home as I rode out the jetlag. It was surreal to read more about the way "race" was constructed in a country where I was a very visible minority. But my curiosity about skin colour and place quickly faded into the background as I reconnected with family—some related, some chosen—and fell into the fold. Austria is not a place I know much about, beyond the people that matter to me there.

Surrounded

I am surrounded
by mountains
and family
places my feet have walked
as a child,
windows I have looked out of,
echoes of laughter,
ping-pong championships,
and the first feelings of growing up

I am surrounded
by people who
have witnessed my growth
in a place
that is magical

Not because of
the scenery,
although beautiful,
but because
I feel connected
to this small group of people,
my mother's people

And a part of me relaxes

So, What Happened?

I went to Austria
with hackles
feeling prickly
like I had to protect myself
and my child
or at least...
be ready for it

I went not knowing
how it would feel,
how I would feel,
and watching my daughter
like a hawk
wondering what it would be like
for her
(my precious brown-skinned child
who for months, years,
has wanted to be blonde
and white)
to be surrounded by people
she looks nothing like

What would that do to her
fragile sense of self?

Instead, what I found
was family
memories
and a sense of place

that I don't
have anywhere else
in the world

I was surrounded
at a large table
with people who are
woven into my life.
There was laughter
and love,
and it felt like home

I discovered that
it is the memories,
the inexplicable something
that comes with those,
that contributes to my sense of home
of place
of relief

Like a magic invisible rope
that when I put my arms
around these people
feels like
it gets stronger
pulls us closer

We look nothing alike

I don't look like I belong here

And yet...
they are my family

I am home

Belonging...At Work

What I learned on my trip to Austria was not what I thought I would. My biggest lesson was about belonging and its link to being seen and known. It was a simple lesson, *one that I teach*!

But I had to experience it in this country for myself. I had to sink into the experience of not looking like I fit and having it not matter because I belonged.

Belonging comes from connection, from shared moments, from community.

This is what I help people and organizations to create. Inclusion and belonging are not something we can *do*. They are *outcomes* of the energy and investment we make in our people.

When I walked into my aunt's home in Austria, I was surrounded by shared memories.

It's true; we don't know everything about each other. We seldom see each other. We haven't had a lot of hard conversations, but because we have shared moments, we have something to hang onto that can accompany us through those.

My cousins and I had an interesting conversation about the debate over the name of a dessert (literally, a chocolate and vanilla dessert called "Moors in a shirt"). And on a tour of the rehab centre that my cousin runs, I did point out that having a cross in the room meant for anyone to use as a sacred space was at odds with the intention. I didn't hide. And they seemed to listen. Maybe if I was there longer, and if my German was stronger, our different life experiences, lenses, and perspectives would clash. But those can feel different and can be navigated differently when there is a connection.

In workplaces, we need to build community. We spend so much time together at work (or in virtual workspaces recently); we have to also create shared memories—and not just with the folks we look like, share a role with, or think we have things in common with. Leaders need to make the time to cultivate a sense of community and learning so people can show up, be themselves, and have a safety net for when things get heated, dicey, and when we need to confront tough issues or situations.

Questions to Ponder

1. How are you building community in your workplace?

2. What is the "culture fit" that employees are expected to have?

3. What could it look like if you considered what people bring to the table that is unique and meaningful (their "culture add"[41]) instead?

---

[41] Credit to Allyson Byrd, for coining this phrase.

CHAPTER 12

Both/And

This is a new place for me. Forty-nine years of either/or is a lot of conditioning to overcome.

And yet I'm sure this is better. I *know* it is, deep in my soul. I'm sure we need to hold this place in the world so we can heal, just as I know I need to hold this place in my body so I can heal.

My daughter has a sign that she made on her window; it's been there for a while. It says,

"Everyone is awesome in their own way. Even when you are black and white."

For a long time, I wanted to correct the grammar. "Black *or* white, sweetheart," I wanted to say.

When we came home from our trip to Austria, it suddenly dawned on me; there is no grammatical error. She was sending me a message. She was sending the world a message.

Black *and* white.

It's no mistake.

Interestingly, as soon as this new energy settled in me—this both/and—she stopped saying she wanted to be white. It was like something in her was calling this out in me, and she no longer needed to. She now calls herself black. And she has often told me she thinks I'm white—no matter how many times I show her we are pretty much the same shade of brown.

I gather she sees and feels my cultural background, not my skin. My experience, not my melanin. She is wise like that. She's not wrong.

And it's okay now.

Mostly.

I know who I am.

Just DNA?

'No race'
should make me
more free
and in some ways
it does

Reminds me of our
common humanity
connects me
with everyone
in a DNA dance

And in other ways
I feel more lost
have less of a tether
to my families
than I did before

I am a product
of chance
random sequencing
due to ancestral
adaptation

True
I wouldn't be
the colour I am
without my parents

But they didn't
give it to me
it didn't come wrapped
in two packages
merged

My skin colour
was created
as part
of who I am

It's mine

Six months after my "ah hah" moment in Winnipeg, I found myself in Texas, USA co-facilitating a session on "race" with two colleagues, Valerie Sheppard and Dr. Ganz Ferrance. Our goal was to help folks understand that "race" isn't real, and the *impact* of racism and unconscious bias. It was a starting point for an organization all three of us belong to. Having a view of the Robert E. Lee hotel across the street as we met with the board of directors was fitting and bizarre at the same time.

We had spent months planning and had the help of a few volunteers to do a role-play where we could hear some of the ways we duck out of conversations about "race." We had a room for folks to come and chat with us afterwards. We created a space around the "actors" so they could debrief. We got the conversation going. It was powerful. And, we missed creating a space for folks who are black and people of colour (like us) who needed some quiet time afterwards, together, to *sit, talk, share, and regroup.* That hurt my heart and gave me pause; it reminded me of who I am—and who I am not. It flung me backwards, and sunk me into shame, again.

How could I have missed that? Given the awareness I have cultivated and speak about, how did I (how did we), fail to remember to create a safe space for people who are black and people of colour to gather after our session? I felt sick. And it took me away from the beauty we had created through our work, a blemish on an otherwise valuable experience.

Not Yet...

Nose pressed
to the glass
again

My people
not my people

Shattered
by the things
I do not know

Crushed
by the impact
of the things
I miss

Still waiting
to step over
the divide
and be home
there

Instead of owning
where I am
gifts and failings
that make me
me

And using all of it
to help us heal

All of us

Just the Beginning

So much left
to learn
in my new shoes

Owning what I do not know
using what I'm privy to
standing in my place
not the place I have tried to be in
the shoes I have tried to fill
for legitimacy
to match how others see me

I'm stepping into who I am,
out of who you think I am

holding both
and neither
at the same time

Making space
for something new

This experience was painful, and the spectre of "not black enough" snuck back in for a visit until my friend and colleague Ben Gioia wisely pointed out that this experience was a reminder of continual learning and growth. He was right. I have found a place, but I don't get to rest. It actually requires that I show up *more*. The energy I save from not running between black and white or having to choose a side is being transformed into holding both, in all their complexity, and creating a circle of love.

This Time, You Cried

Waiting for your approval
and fearing your rejection
I stay away
until I cannot wait
any longer

Your tears
tell me of healing
and of pain

Your words
wash over me
and surround my heart

My tears
allow me to sink
into the pain
of never
and the hope of
one day

One day
when we are all
connected
my pain
our pain
will end…

Both

If I let you name me as black
then I lose myself
in all I do not know
about a people
cultures
that have given me my colour

If I discount
what I <u>do</u> know
the knowledge that comes
with my melanin
I make you—and me—invisible
again

If I don't own
my whiteness
I erase you by my omissions
and make spaces less safe

This path is mine

No roadmap

Pain
awareness
and love
will guide me
and I will be a bridge

Strong
trampled

necessary
leading us to a new place

Standing alone

Not one or the other
but part of both

Bridging the divide

Both/And at Work

It's tempting to snap back to what we have known, see things the way we have always seen them, and do things the way we have always done them. This path is no exception. I have to remind myself that there is nothing to prove, that I'm okay as I am, that I have something to offer, *as me, just me, as black and white as I am.*

When we are not allowed to be who we are, we lose out. And those around us lose out as well.

Because we are not afforded the opportunity to share what we know; we think we have to come up with something better, something *else.* This is tragic in any circumstance, and in the workplace, this kills innovation and creativity, prevents us from managing risks, and undermines opportunity.

Being all of who you are in a workplace is only possible when the space is safer—safer to show up, safer to speak up, safer to make mistakes, and safer to ask questions. Amy Edmondson calls this psychological safety[42]. There will be many common elements to this safety, and we also have to remember diversity and the impact of who we are on what we need, and the barriers we face – in this case about things like speaking up, asking questions, giving feedback – due to identity, lived experience, assumptions, stereotypes and of course power dynamics related to position but also to identity. When we create safety, we create a space where mistakes are okay, questions are expected, and learning is the name of the game. These are the precursors to inclusion because when we recognize that we are connected even

---

[42]   Amy Edmondson's book is called *The Fearless Organization*

though we are different we *want* to learn, we *want* to ask questions, and we *want* to build community.

Both/and means holding space, acknowledging blind spots, listening to and valuing multiple truths, realities, and experiences, creating safer spaces for conversation, and making room to learn.

As we move through change as an organization (or a community) however, we must remember and address the *differential impact* of a commitment to diversity and inclusion (and even more so to anti-racism and anti-oppression) on people who are black and people of colour (and on other Historically Disadvantaged Groups as well). Simply put, the ride is different. As a result (and as an acknowledgment), sometimes we need to create separate spaces, and conversations need to happen separately to build a bridge and create the future possibility of having conversations together.

The work of inclusion never ends. There will always be something new, something more. We will continually bump up against things we don't know, things we thought we knew, or things we thought we understood but don't quite. There will always be new situations that we haven't experienced before.

But when we hold both/and instead of either/or, we have the opportunity to travel there together.

This requires cultural humility.[43]

There will always be something we don't know, can't know, or won't know. And that's okay. This is

---

[43] Cultural Humility—a documentary explaining the concept by Vivian Chavez https://www.youtube.com/watch?v=SaSH-LbS1V4w&t=12s Sourced: September 6, 2020

why questions are so important—and why creating the container for asking them is so powerful.

When we hold both/and, we have an entry point for a possibility, an acknowledgment, a conversation, without the weight of having to choose a side.

The goal of a both/and space is to move us away from polarization toward greater connection, seeing more, and ultimately, greater belonging—and change.

In that space, there is room.

And we all win.

Questions to Ponder

1. How safe is your workplace? And how do you know?

2. How can you cultivate safer spaces for people to share and talk and safer spaces to learn and grow?

3. How do you encourage learning?

4. What is an example of both/and that you can begin to explore?

Hello

Hello
I said to myself
as I looked in the mirror
and saw myself
for the first time

Hello
I see you

I am here
tall,
brown

With my ancestors
at my back
surrounding me

Both sides
black
and white
but mingling
healing
laughing

Together

Breathe

Let's do this
I'm ready now...

NOW WHAT?

We've come to the end of the book. But really, it's only the beginning of what's next.

We are living in interesting times.

I started writing this book long before George Floyd's murder was seen on video around the world. By the time you read it, who knows where that moment of awareness and consciousness-raising will have taken us.

I hope we come so far that we can't remember what the world looked like before. For the better. I hope that conversations about "race" and racism have been deeper and lead to action—action we can see and feel. I hope the sign on my daughter's window is coming true.

"Everyone is awesome in their own way, even when they are black and white."

If you're inspired and want to keep diversity and inclusion on your radar, please sign up for my **weekly newsletter** on my website: http://annemarieshrouder.com/.

If you are a leader in a company or organization, you can find information about my **Inclusive Leadership Program** here: http://annemarieshrouder. com/inclusive-leadership-program/

And I invite you to check out **Around the Fire**—a community I'm creating to help us connect across difference and experience the beauty in that connection: https://www.aroundfire.com

These are exciting times! And we are *all* needed around the fire.

Looking forward to seeing you there.

Annemarie

ACKNOWLEDGEMENT AND THANKS

So many people have been instrumental on my journey. Some have been mentioned in these pages (some by name and some with pseudonyms). I would like to specifically acknowledge and thank:

H.S.—for cracking me open to
my pain, so I explored it
André—for helping me access my
pain, so I could write it
Joseph—for reminding me that either/or never works
Ben—for helping me own my story
and send it out into the world
Dany—for helping me see it had to be me

And to my amazing child, who has taught me that
"Everyone is awesome in their own way,
even when they are black and white."
I love you, sweetheart.

CPSIA information can be obtained
at www.ICGtesting.com
Printed in the USA
LVHW020030110222
710851LV00009B/155/J